REMBRANDT
AND
THE GOSPEL

W. A. VISSER 'T HOOFT

LIVING AGE BOOKS
published by MERIDIAN BOOKS, INC.   *New York*

W. A. VISSER 'T HOOFT

*W(illem) A(dolf) Visser 't Hooft was born in
Haarlem, Holland, on September 20, 1900. He earned
his doctorate at the University of Leyden in 1928,
and received the degree of D.D. at the University of
Aberdeen in 1939. An ordained minister of the
Netherlands Reformed Church, Dr. Visser 't Hooft is a
leader in the ecumenical movement, an extensive
traveler, and author of numerous widely read books on
the Protestant church and its place in world society.
He has been general secretary of the World Council of
Churches since 1938.*

Translated by K. Gregor Smith from the German text,
REMBRANDTS WEG ZUM EVANGELIUM, *revised
by the author.*

A LIVING AGE BOOK

Published by Meridian Books, Inc. August 1960
First printing July 1960
Reprinted by arrangement with The Westminster Press
Library of Congress Catalog Card Number: 58-5487
Manufactured in the United States of America

Contents

Contents

List of Illustrations

7

CHAPTER ONE

Rembrandt's Pilgrimage

★ ★ ★

R EMBRANDT was born in Leyden in 1606. In all likelihood it was his mother, whom he repeatedly painted with her Bible, who introduced him to Holy Scripture. From 1613 he attended the grammar school, where the Bible as well as the Classics were studied daily. In 1620 his father planned to send him to the university; but Rembrandt's one and only passion was painting. For three years he worked in a studio in Leyden, and thereafter was for several months the pupil of Pieter Lastman in Amsterdam. There he was introduced to the Italian style of painting, whose predominant themes were historical and biblical. But we can hardly describe this kind of religious painting as biblical, for it is concerned with the beautiful stories of the Bible rather than with its meaning.

From 1625 till 1632 he worked independently in Leyden, and sought his own personal mode of expression. When the statesman Huygens paid him a visit during that time, and pressed him to go to Italy, he replied that he had no time for travelling, and that, besides, there were enough Italian masterpieces to be seen in Holland. A great many of his paintings from that period deal with biblical themes: Balaam, Samson, David and Goliath, Tobit, Simeon, the expulsion from the Temple, Judas, St Paul. Strong contrasts, great passions, heroic figures are his main themes. Rembrandt was in search of the grandiose, and the biblical world appeared to him as a world of supermen.

In 1632 he left his native town and settled in Amsterdam, the centre of intellectual life in Holland. His reputation grew rapidly. He executed commissioned portraits with remarkable technical skill, but without inwardness or depth. Soon the miller's son was able to marry a girl from a very good family, Saskia van Uylenburch (1634). His income enabled him to give free rein to his passion for collecting paintings, engravings and oriental curiosities. His collection grew to be 'one of the most remarkable that ever existed'.[1]

Judging by his self-portraits, the Rembrandt of that time was a passionate, pleasure-seeking, somewhat showy man, to whom the whole world was open, and life itself a feast of light and colour. The baroque style fascinated him in virtue of its splendour and dramatic fulness; but the artist still wanted to remain true to himself. In the long run he could not rest satisfied with imitation of the great Italian or Flemish masters. So he tried to translate the baroque style into a more realistic and less pompous language. The result was ambiguous, for though his painting of this period no longer displayed the aristocratic attitude and the ecclesiastical pomp of international baroque, it still retained the dynamic, or rather rhetorical, element. In one of the few letters that have been preserved (1639), he describes his artistic aim as 'the most natural liveliness',[2] and these words describe very well indeed the peculiar combination in his style of the naturalism of the Netherlands with the gesturing of the baroque.

The influence upon him of his great contemporary Rubens can be easily recognized. Several paintings and etchings of the time are evidence of his—generally not very successful—attempts to unite in one whole the weighty, almost boastful art of Rubens with his own manner, which was always direct and genuine.

During this period Rembrandt tried his hand at mythological themes, but his classical figures impress us as strangely unheroic. The picture of Saskia and himself,* painted in the grand style, reminds us disagreeably of an untidy masquerade.[3]

Even by this time he had attempted great biblical themes. Wherein lay the attraction of the Bible for him? Mainly in the lively, dramatic, and even sensational themes which it offered. Several times he handled the story of Samson (but after 1642 this theme disappeared from his work), but in a theatrical rather than a truly biblical style. *Christ at Emmaus** (1629, Jacquemart Andrée, Paris) becomes a noisy scene. In *The Raising of Lazarus** (1632) Jesus appears as a sorcerer working a physical rather than a spiritual miracle. *The Annunciation to the Shepherds* inspires an etching where everything is movement, but nobody really listens to the glad tidings of the Nativity. *Ecce Homo** (1635) shows a Christ who has been represented under the influence of Guido Reni's sentimentalism, and who faces a mob of Jews looking more like robbers than religious leaders.

We cannot really describe the Rembrandt of that period as a biblical painter. His excited style, the exaggeration of the gestures and the stressing of the rhetorical do not rise out of the spirit of the Bible. The mixture of naturalism and baroque produces religious painting which seems even more worldly than the art of the Renaissance and the Counter-Reformation. This is especially clear in the pictures *Resurrection* (1636), and *Ascension* (1639), which were painted for Prince Frederick Henry of Orange (Munich), where the inner spiritual movement is quite overwhelmed by the externals. The artist himself, however, was not conscious of this. In a letter of the year 1639, on the contrary, he expressed himself as highly satisfied with his success in 'reproducing the great shock felt by the guards, in the representation of the Ascension'.

Up to the year 1642 Rembrandt's life was like a triumphal procession. Then Saskia died, leaving him alone with his year-old son Titus. Rembrandt began to be acquainted with grief and loneliness. In the same year he finished the *Night Watch*. This painting was like a revolutionary manifesto for a new programme. He had discovered a new and deep dimension, which he expressed in terms of the newly won charm of *chiaroscuro*. This certainly won him his independence, but he had to pay the price. Commissions became rarer, and people were affronted by this headstrong artist whose work showed that he was less concerned with facial likeness than with his own bold experiments in light and shade.

In the same years, 1642 to 1648, a Copernican revolution took place in Rembrandt's life. His self-portraits during this period show how great and profound that inner change was. Self-complacency, self-assertion, lust for pleasure disappear; his eyes become deeper and speak of suffering and loneliness. But at the same time a new strength appears in his features which is drawn from his victory over inner restlessness. We do not quite know how he won this victory; but we realize that he must have gone through many hours of sorrow. The deplorable episode of his intimate relations with Geertghe Dircx, who came into his house to look after little Titus, and must have been a coarse woman, can be understood only as a despairing reaction against his loneliness. It was in this dark time that he made his deeper discoveries. In 1645 he painted a number of pictures representing the story of the child Jesus, and here for the first time we meet with the great simplicity and the great concentrated stillness which are in harmony with the story of the Bible. Now Rembrandt realized that this delicate expression alone was suited to the spiritual world into which he was entering.

At this time the Holy Family took the central place in his mind (nine times we find the Holy Family and nine times the Flight into Egypt). In Joseph, Mary and the Child we do not find certain 'types' or other-worldly beings, as with the painters of the Renaissance or the baroque style. They live our life, and are a challenge to the idealizing art of previous generations. Rembrandt finally turned his back on the glorification of man which had become the classical ideal, and which reached its zenith in baroque art. Thus he shows us that he has learned that it is a humble thing to be a man. From this time the beautiful ceased to be an end in itself for him. He realized that beauty must serve something higher, namely truth, or else it is in danger of becoming an empty shell, falsifying the reality of life. If beauty accepts this part, it acquires a new substance through which the eternal shines. This new discovery found its expression chiefly in Rembrandt's biblical works. Does this not imply that it is the Bible which compels this revolution in his entire conception of life and art?

The year 1648 has a special significance in Rembrandt's life. Was this because in that year the protracted war with Spain came to an end? The peace treaty was signed in Münster, and the Netherlands, and Amsterdam in particular, celebrated the return of peace after eighty troubled years of war. Painters and poets joined in the general enthusiasm. Van der Helst painted his famous *Banquet of the Civic Guard* which reflects in magnificent style a mood of success, comfort and pomp, combined with external conformity. Vondel published grandiloquent poems in keeping with the taste of the time.

Was Rembrandt also to give way, and thus secure easy success? No, for he felt a call to greater things. His harvest time had come. From this time on, nothing was to divert him from his path. The spiritual discoveries he had made, the inspiration he had received, were henceforth expressed in his pictures. If he is frowned upon by some, regarded as a heretic, a trespasser against the laws of art, what did he care? He had to make his confession in his own language.

At the very moment of the supreme triumph of baroque art, when the Jesuit Bernini in Italy was putting the finishing touches to his *Santa Teresa*—a subtly devised mixture of erotic and Christian elements —in Rembrandt's studio an art was born whose aim was to represent the biblical events in the spirit of the Bible.

1648 was Rembrandt's year of grace: the year of the *Disciples of Emmaus* of the Louvre and of Copenhagen, the year of two pictures and eight drawings of *The Good Samaritan*, and of the beginning of a series of Portraits of Christ (about eight between 1648 and

1650). It is difficult to analyse the Christ of those years. At first glance the portrait seems to be of a Jewish rabbi—the deepest and most delicate portrait possible. But then you feel there is a mystery. This Christ is far from impressing us by his majesty. On the contrary, he is 'without form nor beauty', he 'does not raise his voice'; but he asks us a question, a commanding question.

After 1648 difficulties increased. The artist had spent too much money on his collections, and commissions became fewer. His son Titus tried to help him, and stayed with him without any reproaches; as did young Hendrickje Stoffels, a woman of admirable self-sacrificing love. Rembrandt could not marry her, being bound by Saskia's will, which in the event of a second marriage forced him to repay to Titus the amount of his mother's inheritance. Where was he to find money? In 1651 or 1652 his daughter Cornelia was born, and this illegal situation made his social position more difficult than ever.

In 1656 he was faced with bankruptcy and had to sell all his possessions. Thus an indescribably rich collection of paintings, engravings, drawings and *objets d'art* from many countries was scattered. There was no friend or patron in that great mercantile city to spare the artist that heavy loss. Only two books are mentioned in the inventory: Josephus's *History of the Jews,* and 'an old Bible'.

In those years Rembrandt became increasingly the painter of the Bible. He was no longer concerned with the dramatic stories, but with the content of the Bible. He worked at two sets of etchings, the first about *Jesus' Boyhood* (five pictures), and the other about the

15

Passion. Among the first is that moving etching where we see the boy Jesus taking his parents by the hand and leading them towards a destiny of which Mary already has an inkling. The other series contains the most impressive etching the artist had so far produced, *The Three Crosses*, of which it has been said that 'Only once, in Rembrandt's vision, has the Christian imagination truly dwelt on Golgotha.'[4]

But Rembrandt was working at other themes as well: *Christ Teaching* (twice), *Jesus and the Woman of Samaria* (six times), *Christ at Gethsemane* (eight times—there is only one Gethsemane among his earlier works, in 1645) and above all *Christ at Emmaus* (nine times). The last *Emmaus*, of 1661* (Louvre), which is much less known than that of 1648 (also in the Louvre), stresses the development since 1627. From 'natural liveliness' he has advanced to a supernatural quietness, but this supernatural quality is expressed only indirectly, and no more than hinted.

The Old Testament was also the source of numerous themes: *Jacob's Blessing* (1656), *Abraham Entertaining the Angels* (1656), *Abraham Sacrificing Isaac* (1655), *King David* (1651) and *Saul and David* (about 1657). All these pictures show an increasing concentration on what is most important, and the omission of anything which might distract the attention. Rembrandt is no longer the artist who is fascinated in turn by religious themes and artistic experiments. He is completely in the thrall of biblical thought. If Rembrandt is regarded as the most biblical of all painters, he owes this reputation mainly to the works of this period.

During 1661 the master worked chiefly at a series of studies of the apostles and evangelists. His *Evangelist*

*Matthew** of the Louvre, in which he interprets the meaning of the inspiration of the Bible, is the most famous of this series. And from his self-portrait as *St Paul,** probably in the same series, we may understand the development he has gone through. Nothing remains of the youthful, self-satisfied conqueror of earlier days. But matured in grief, he no longer demands anything from life; his gaze is directed towards the secrets of another world.

In that last phase of his life Rembrandt lived in seclusion. Few friends were left to him. Hendrickje died in 1662, Titus in 1668. The artist's last works tell of his effort to speak the unspeakable. Everything which is merely anecdotal has disappeared. He gives us one work which sums up his entire pilgrimage: *The Return of the Prodigal Son.* This son, who delivers himself into his father's hands, surrenders himself to his verdict, is no figure from a parable. But he is Rembrandt himself, he is man, at all times and in all places, who seeks and finds his father's open arms.

In the year of his death it became terribly apparent that Rembrandt had failed in the struggle for existence but also that he found strength and comfort in the gospel even in—or rather through—his need. He had again fallen into the hands of a moneylender and had to work for him.[5] What did he do? A series of etchings of the Passion, and a picture representing Simeon with the Christ Child. When he died, the Simeon picture stood unfinished in his studio. He too could depart in peace, for his eyes had seen the salvation. An inventory of his goods and chattels was drawn up once more. The list is short. Under No. 22 the lawyer noted the only book found among his possessions: a Bible.

17

CHAPTER TWO

The Painter of the Bible

★ ★ ★

CONTEMPORARY painter and pupil of Rembrandt's[1] remarks bitterly that since the churches are closed to Dutch painters 'their best careers' are spoilt for most of them, and they content themselves with 'lowly things' or 'futilities' for their subjects. This judgment may be exaggerated or superficial, since portraits, landscapes and still life may also have their deeper meaning, and do not deserve such contempt. But it is true all the same that in Rembrandt's time great religious themes play an inferior part and that apart from his own school Dutch painters of the seventeenth century rarely take them for their subjects. Not that the Dutch Protestants went so far as to condemn religious painting as a whole; on the contrary, we know that it had a ready market. But the Church did not provide any commissions, and private people mainly ordered portraits. So a painter had no reason to choose religious subjects unless he did so of his own inclination. 'The choice of the theme was left to the decision of the artist; he shaped it after his own judgment; no criticism of the patron influenced the execution. The advantages arising out of such freedom amply compensated for everything the Calvinist spirit suppressed by abandoning the tradition of Madonnas and Legends of Saints.'[2]

In his choice of a subject for his work Rembrandt always surprises us by his love of the Bible. This man who in 145 paintings (out of about 650), 70 etchings (out of about 300), and 575 drawings (out of 1,250 to 1,500), took biblical themes and treated all of them in an individual manner, did indeed live with the Bible. In this regard the drawings are particularly enlightening because they are mostly not destined for the public. They are like the pages of a diary where all through his life Rembrandt noted down the discoveries he made in the Bible.

In what way does the artist translate the Scriptures? We have seen—and shall see it confirmed again and again—that the Rembrandt of the forties, fifties and sixties had a different relation to the Bible from the young Rembrandt. His work reflects his development, not only leading him to choose different subjects, but also shaping old themes in a new way.

As a young man, Rembrandt looked for the dramatic. The Scriptures were an excellent source of stories full of tension and movement. It was in that period that he conceived the highly baroque pictures of Balaam and Samson, and the miracles he depicts are in reality sorcery. But that does not last. From 1642 onwards, in his loneliness, he discovered the meaning of the message which contains the key to human existence. From that time he no longer sought to exploit the Bible; he tried to interpret it. In his mature years Rembrandt became the servant of the Word of God. He no longer placed himself between that Word and the spectator, nor directed attention to his technical devices and the skill of his means of expression. He wanted to let the gospel speak for itself.

Nothing in this regard is more revealing than to compare the manner of the young Rembrandt, when he paints themes like *The Raising of Lazarus** or *Ecce Homo** or *Christ at Emmaus**, with his later manner, about 1650, when he takes up the same themes once more.

Neumann is right when he says that no other religious pictures are so little influenced by ecclesiastical considerations, and so wholly biblical as those of Rembrandt.[3] The mature artist wants no commentary for the Bible other than the Bible itself. He remains independent of any tradition. But independence does not mean indifference or hostility. He knows his predecessors and often borrows from them an idea, an attitude or an illuminating thought. But his conception of the biblical message is always personal, he never feels bound by any precedent. He never grants the right to anyone to force a particular interpretation upon him.

In his *History of Religious Art since the Council of Trent*[4] Emile Mâle stresses the fact that painters of Catholic countries were not allowed to choose themes from the Bible themselves. Their theme was prescribed. 'So the artist did not need to invent anything. The subjects demanded of him corresponded to the religious sentiment of his time: everywhere the Church was present in them.'

Thus practically all official religious painting was restricted to the traditional iconography and certain selected scenes from the Bible. In Rembrandt's time there was in existence a kind of canon which provided the painter with a list of themes. Certain themes belonged to the official treasure of Christian art; others were omitted. Besides this the point of view from which the subject was to be treated was clearly laid down. Recent studies have shown with what loyalty, even a sense of routine, painters have often followed those laws. But Rembrandt is quite the opposite. When he represents a biblical story, it has come alive, and real, for him; the mature Rembrandt has himself seen and heard something in the story.

Thus we see in his work a far-reaching reduction. Innumerable religious themes which had been added in the tradition of the Church to the biblical themes proper find no more room in his work. But at the same time there is a liberation. In their liturgical selections the Middle Ages left little room for the Bible story itself: only four parables, very few scenes from the life of Jesus, even fewer from the Old Testament and principally those events which are regarded as pre-figurations of the New Testament. The Counter-Reformation was dominated by polemical and didactic aims, and had put all the stress on subjects connected with the Church, without being concerned with the Bible as a whole. For Rembrandt, on the other hand, the Bible alone determines the subject. For that reason his painting is the first example in the history of art of work inspired by the biblical message in all its richness.

Rembrandt read the *whole* Bible. None of the important series of biblical pictures of other painters comprises the whole Bible in this way. From what other painter's work can we publish the Bible in pictures?[5] Fra Angelico confined himself to the New Testament. Dürer represents only four scenes from the Old Testament, so does Rubens; and what is known as

Raphael's Bible is only illustrations from the Old Testament painted by Raphael and his pupils to which four or five pictures from the life of Jesus are added. The other painters of the sixteenth and seventeenth centuries are content to follow the tradition. Thus Rembrandt is the only great painter not only of the Netherlands but also of the whole world to deserve the name of a biblical painter, for he roams through the Bible from beginning to end, and gives us what he discovers.

But we may go even further. Rembrandt not only looks for themes for his pictures in the Bible, he also interprets the texts of Scripture. He by no means restricts himself to general illustration of one story or another, but he presents a special moment, he interprets a certain verse. Hence the names given to the various paintings cannot express their full meaning. We must always go back to the text on which they are based.

For instance, when Rembrandt tells the story of Hagar, he portrays six different scenes: Sarah leading Hagar to Abraham, Sarah complaining about Hagar, Hagar at the well on the way to Sur, the expulsion of Hagar, Hagar in the desert, the angel appearing to Hagar. In his account of Joseph, too, we can take part in all the main events of that tempestuous existence. We see all the scenes of David's drama. Nor is the temptation of Jesus a static subject, but the unrolling of a dramatic action. Gethsemane is seen from very different sides, whether the stress lies on the 'sorrow unto death', on the prayer 'not as I will, but as thou wilt', or on the reproaches to the sleeping disciples.

But all this has not petrified into a system. Rembrandt did not work in series. He only showed what he had heard in the message of the Bible, he only painted what he had 'seen'.

Does this mean that Rembrandt treated *all* the great biblical themes? Certainly not. The 'Rembrandt Bibles' published in Holland and Germany show that there are few books of the Bible with which he has not been concerned, and that he has dealt with many subjects which have been deliberately left out by the iconographic tradition. We note, however, that certain themes frequently recur, while others are missing. We do not intend to enumerate them, but it may serve as an example to note that he treated the story of Abraham thirty-one times, the parable of the Good Samaritan fifteen times, Emmaus eighteen times, whereas he did not handle at all such famous themes of mediaeval painting as the *Last Judgment,* the *Parable of the Ten Virgins, The Rich Man and Lazarus,* or themes popular in baroque painting such as the *Transfiguration,* the *Power of the Keys,* and the *Wedding of Cana.*

The inventory of Rembrandt's collections shows that he possessed engravings of the entire works of Titian, Lucas of Leyden, and Raphael. Thus he was very probably able to study three of the most famous representations of Mary Magdalen every day.[6] He certainly knew the *Transfigurations* of Raphael and Rubens. He owned a *Rich Man and Lazarus* by Palma Vecchio. Those works never inspired him to make his own version of the themes. Why not? The mature Rembrandt represented only 'what he had seen and heard', what he had understood in such a way that he could hand it on.

So the question arises whether we may not elicit Rembrandt's beliefs from his choice of subjects. This question has received detailed attention from Hans Martin Rotermund.[7] He names as the chief omissions from Rembrandt's work the story of Whitsun, Old Testament prefigurations, the Revelation of St John, and the life of St Paul. There is no doubt that the first three of these themes play no part in Rembrandt's work. But it is not true that St Paul is of little or no interest to Rembrandt. From his earlier period there are four paintings, one etching and three drawings representing themes from the life of St Paul, from his later life three paintings. What is even more important, Rembrandt identified himself with St Paul in such a way that he actually depicted himself as St Paul. This painting of 1661 (Collection de Bruyn)* shows most clearly of all the self-portraits of the later years how Rembrandt had detached himself from the world and turned towards the things that are eternal. He who has seen the look on this face will not easily forget it.[8] He is St Paul; but he is also Rembrandt. Both have heard the word, 'My grace is sufficient for thee.'

Rotermund names other themes which play a special part in Rembrandt's work. He rightly emphasizes how Rembrandt in dealing with the Old Testament chooses themes connected not with the struggles of the people of the covenant but with the individual human being meeting God. In his representations of the New Testament we notice his special interest in the teaching and healing Christ, his preference for the humanity of the Mother of Jesus,[9] and his presentation of Jesus' temptation and tribulation in its extreme form of mortal dereliction.[10]

These are notable observations. The question remains, what inferences may be drawn from them.

Rotermund believes this selection to be characteristic-
ally Mennonite. (The followers of Menno rejected
infant baptism and sought to create a 'pure' community of faithful believers.) This conclusion would be
justified if the themes omitted by Rembrandt were
really alien to the Mennonite world, and if the themes
he preferred were not acceptable to those of the
Reformed faith. But that is not so. We give the following examples. In Mennonite circles emphasis is laid on
the influence of the Holy Spirit, so that we should
expect a Mennonite painter to pay special attention to
Whitsun. Nor is it true that Rembrandt's relation to
the Old Testament makes a Mennonite impression.
On the contrary, the Mennonites much prefer to deal
with the New Testament, as is shown in their various
creeds. The Old Testament is regarded as the 'shadow'
of the New Covenant.[11] For Rembrandt, however, the
Old Testament has a direct, 'contemporary' meaning.
Nor can it be said that those of the Reformed faith
interpreted the Old Testament merely as a mirror of
their own national history.[12] The Reformed professor
of theology Jacobus Revius, in his first book of poems
on *Divine History*, has given us many poems which are
concerned with the personal decision of faith, on the
basis of the Old Testament stories. To Reformed
believers the Old Testament is primarily a book of
revelation, and only secondarily a book which mirrors
the destiny of a nation. Further, to see Christ as a
teacher, and not solely as the mediator, is of course
not only 'Mennonite'; it is equally a Reformed
characteristic.

Can there be a more objective display of Rembrandt's 'theological' attitude than in his presentation

of the sacraments? Rotermund believes that he has found here the proofs he seeks. He stresses that the Last Supper has little place in Rembrandt's work, and that it is replaced by the supper at Emmaus; that the foot-washing was depicted several times, and that, moreover, adult baptism is a favourite subject.

It is indeed strange that Rembrandt represents the institution of the Last Supper in only a few drawings, taking Leonardo's famous picture as a model but at the same time transforming it. On the other hand we know how absorbed he was by the Emmaus story. What is the significance of this? Obermüller gives the best explanation.[13] He writes: 'Instead of the representations of the Last Supper, which is an interesting dramatic subject for a painter, especially in the form given to it by Leonardo, Rembrandt, foregoing another variety of this motif, presents the story of Emmaus,' and he adds that a kind of theological (or perhaps better a pious) reflection must have been at work. And in fact we feel quite clearly that in the later representations of the Emmaus story the theme is the eternal presence of Christ and the community of believers with him, a theme which is also at the heart of the Last Supper. Hence the reverence and awe of the disciples, which do not arise only (as in the early works) from recognition of their friend and master; rather they are overcome by the fact that the Lord is really alive, really present, and that they may share in his life.

In this consciously or unconsciously, Rembrandt adopted an ancient tradition. St Augustine had interpreted the meal at Emmaus as a communion meal. In Rembrandt's time Hugo Grotius in his *Annotationes* gave 'the mystic interpretation of Luke 24.31, in the ancient tradition, according to which only those truly know Christ who have communion with his body, and that this is established by the breaking of the bread'. Calvin, who wished to explain the words 'plus simplement', called the old exegesis a possible one. That tradition also found an expression in mediaeval iconography.[14] It is not important whether Rembrandt knew that tradition or not. He was undoubtedly convinced that by representing the Emmaus story he was able to express better and more clearly the true meaning of the presence of Christ and of communion with him. Probably a painter's reasons played an important part here too. In painting the institution of the Last Supper, too many motives have to be taken into account—such as the many disciples and the betrayal—which detract from the main theme. The Emmaus meal on the other hand, can be so depicted that only the one decisive idea is expressed (as is especially the case in the two Louvre paintings).

Why this conception of the Supper has to be regarded, as Rotermund thinks, not as Reformed but as Mennonite, is not at all clear. The fact that Holy Communion is sometimes called the feast of the breaking of the bread, does not mean anything, for this is simply based on the New Testament. In the Reformed translation of the Bible a marginal note to Acts 20.7 says that breaking of the bread means communion. And wine as well as bread is of course distributed at Communion by the Mennonites too.[15] The importance of the blood shed for the forgiveness of sins is stressed in their creed no less than the meaning of the breaking of the bread. The fact that the Mennonites have maintained the purity of the Holy Communion more strictly than any other church proves how important the Communion is to them of all people. This plays a great role in their opposition to the Quakers, who do not approve of any sacraments at all.[16]

In the paintings connected with baptism, still less Mennonite influence can be traced.[17] It is remarkable how little interest this theme has for Rembrandt. It is true that John the Baptist is sometimes depicted, but strangely enough (with the exception of the drawing of Christ's baptism) as a preacher and not as a baptizer —though the four Gospels stress his baptizing 'unto remission of sins'. It is also true that Rembrandt several times depicted the baptism of the Ethiopian eunuch, but this was a favourite subject of the Lastman school. In Biestken's New Testament,[18] which was used by the Mennonites, we find in the 'List of the most important articles of faith', under 'baptism'—in proof, of course, that only adult baptism is known in the Bible—the baptisms in Acts enumerated as the most important: Simon Magus, the Ethiopian eunuch, Lydia, Cornelius, the jailer. Of these themes only that of the Ethiopian is treated by Rembrandt. It is even stranger that we have only one study of Christ's baptism, whereas the circumcision was painted, etched or drawn by Rembrandt nine times, and at all periods of his life.[19] If we remember that the circumcision played a great part in the polemics of the Reformed Church against the Mennonites,[20] and that the Reformed defended infant baptism with the argument that 'children should be baptized and sealed with the sign of the covenant, just as formerly children were

circumcised in Israel', we might even draw the conclusion that Rembrandt's great interest in circumcision
is a typical Reformed attitude. Such an argumentation,
however, seems to me to be too uncertain. For it is
perfectly possible that he understood these themes not
in a 'denominational' but in a purely historical manner,
and that here too he saw the true Incarnation of
Christ. At any rate it is clear that there is no Mennonite
influence here.

It is well known that Rembrandt was greatly
attracted to the Book of Tobit. But in the question of
his beliefs we are not much helped by this knowledge,
for in the Reformed as well as the Mennonite community the Old Testament Apocrypha were widely
read. They were printed in the Bibles and recited in the
liturgies. The creed of the Reformed Church taught
that the Church can read 'and draw from them instruc-
tion in matters in conformity with the canonical
writings'. The Synod of Dordrecht had agreed to a
new translation of those books on condition that they
were placed separately at the end of the Bible. The
Icones Biblicae of the Reformed engraver Matthaeus
Merian of Basel, which appeared in Strasbourg between 1625 and 1629, and soon afterwards, in Amsterdam, and which Rembrandt probably knew, includes
in its second part fourteen illustrations of the Apocrypha. The Great Bible, published in 1710, with illustrations by Romeyn de Hooghe and commentary by the
orthodox Reformed pastor Basnage, contains several
pictures of Tobit and Judith. Basnage considered
Tobit to be a historical figure who lived among the
exiled Jews in Nineveh.

All this proves that we cannot construct any

29

'system' from Rembrandt's choice of subjects or his handling of them. Nor could this be expected. He was a painter and not a theologian. He went his own way, which does not mean that he ruled out any stimulus he might receive from his acquaintance with members of the Reformed, the Remonstrant, the Mennonite, the Catholic, the Jewish, or the humanist community. One thing only is certain: he lived with his Bible. He was in truth '*homo unius libri*'. The Bible was the 'backbone of his life, his comfort in his grief and loneliness, his only hope when everything turned against him, his sheet-anchor, his vindication'.[21]

CHAPTER THREE

Christic in Rembrandt's Work

★   ★   ★

IN seventeenth-century official art the story of
Christ became a heroic epic. Towards the end of his
life, in 1634, Rubens painted *Christ carrying the Cross*
(Brussels), which is described by Fromentin in the
following terms: 'For those who can see, it is clear that
with that pageant of mounted troops, those waving
banners, that centurion in armour with the elegant
gesture and with Rubens's own features—that with all
that the execution is forgotten, and we feel we are
witnessing a triumphal procession.'[1]

The Roman Catholic art of the Counter-Reformation desires to convince us that Christ is truly God's
Son. In this it is right. But it wishes to base this conviction on a representation of Christ in which the
resplendence of his divine nature is seen and felt
directly. In this it is wrong and misses its goal. The
true mystery of the Son of God become man and
abased is absent from those representations. The
superman or demi-god depicted there has nothing in
common with the Christ in the form of a servant.
Hence Rubens's pictures of Christ may fill us with awe,
those of Guido Reni with compassion, but they never
confront us with another world, but only with this our
present world. For the divine is not a revised version

of the human, and we do not transform human qualities into divine qualities by heightening, intensifying
and exaggerating them. It is not possible to describe in
this way that intervention in world history where
things were at stake 'which entered not into the heart
of man'.

But does not the art of the Counter-Reformation
glorify Christ's *humility*? It does, but it understands
humility in a moralistic sense. The Bible is concerned
with humiliation, with abasement. For the artists of
the baroque period, Christ's humility serves simply as
a means to make his divinity shine the more brightly.
In the Bible, on the other hand, Christ's divine nature
is veiled by his abasement.

What else does Murillo attempt in his *Baptism of
Christ* (Seville) but to excite our admiration for the
God-man who is so humble that he receives baptism
from John? But does he tell us of the great mystery
of the Christ? There is nothing here to indicate that
we can only believe, not see, that this man is the
Messiah.

Christian art of this kind does not really leave any
room for faith. It has no idea that 'the honour due to
the Son of God did not dwell in outward splendour
and magnificence, nor in the glory of this world,
but that it was of an almost entirely spiritual nature'.[2]
This honour cannot be communicated by direct visible
impressions. It is there *in spite of* what the eye sees.
In truth Renaissance and baroque art leave aside the
proper event of the Incarnation. In place of the Word
become flesh, of the God who descends into the
deepest misery of man, they glorify the Word which
has become beauty, heroism, glorious humanity.

It is a surprising fact that the countries of the Reformation gave the warmest welcome to that art which was so alien to their beliefs. Holmes rightly says that 'the nations which shed their blood for the sake of freedom from Roman doctrine continue to venerate and preserve uncritically the art raised on that very dogma'.[3]

Under the influence of baroque art Rembrandt, too, in his youth thought it appropriate to depict Christ in a grand and dignified manner. We are meant to recognize at first glance in this man the Saviour of the world. Neumann exaggerates when he writes that Rembrandt never tried to glorify Christ by means of his bodily appearance. On the contrary, some works of the earlier period do try to prove the authenticity of Christ's mission by his gesture or look, e.g. the *Christ at Emmaus* of 1629* (Jacquemart Andrée), *The Raising of Lazarus* of 1632,* the *Ecce Homo* of 1636.*

In his later years, however, Rembrandt ceased to depict the Christ resplendent in human glory. The Bible revealed to him the mystery of the Messiah and of his *unknown coming* into the world. Rembrandt realized that the meaning of the Incarnation is not the deification of human nature, but the love of God who abases himself to accept even the form of his creature, the form of a servant. He now knew what was known to Luther, Calvin and Pascal, that the Revelation is not a demonstration of God's power and glory which is at once evident to everybody, but a descent of God which is only intelligible to faith. Luther says: 'To know Christ, that he has become man, and has abased himself so deeply that he looked like the most despised and unworthy of men, afflicted and chastised by God,

(Isa. 53), and all that for our sake—this is the right golden art of Christians and their highest wisdom.'[4] Calvin speaks of the lowliness of the flesh of Christ, which like a veil hides his divine majesty.[5] Pascal writes to Mlle de Roannez: 'As long as he was invisible, he was much easier to know than now that he has shown himself visibly.'[6]

The famous etching of Faustus of the beginning of the fifties is probably a further proof that Rembrandt really understood the mystery of the hiddenness of God's revelation. Doctor Faustus sees a magic circle in whose centre the symbol of Christ (I.N.R.I.) appears. If we are right in understanding the words forming the circle as an anagram, we obtain the sentence, *'Tangas larga, latet Amor; Adam te adgeram'*, 'Things unfolded (earthly) you may touch, but (heavenly) love is hidden. Man, I shall lead you thither.'[7] These words do harmonize surprisingly with what we have discovered in Rembrandt's work. It is the love of God which is hidden under the veil of Christ's humanity, and hence only reveals itself to faith.

Since Rembrandt knew of this incognito of Christ, the Christ in his work no longer bears any resemblance to a figure from a heroic epic poem, or a model of touching humility. He is the Messiah of Isa. 53, 'Without form or comeliness'. He is born without splendour: the three figures of the Holy Night[8] are poor and forsaken and have nothing to do with a 'Trinity on earth'. Gethsemane is the theatre of a struggle for life and death, and Gologotha is the place of ultimate dereliction. Rembrandt is as realistic as the Gospels, and in no way relieves the events of their terror, their brutality and their scandal. After Jesus' burial, everything is over, and the disciples are left without any hope. Against that background of the lowest depths of humanity Rembrandt causes the miracle of Emmaus to shine out brightly. For here really is a miracle, such an unambiguous deed of God that it is impossible to add any romantic or sentimental element to it.

What means does the artist employ to render this ineffable drama of God which takes place in the midst of human existence? According to Holmes,[9] none of the various representations made by the artist reveals Christ's personality in a direct way. Only by the manner in which those around him react, is it possible for his presence to be recognized. The novelty in the technique of this painter of the Bible consists in men discovering that this insignificant figure, without beauty or power, is the one *on whom everything depends*. These people listen to him as if their lives were at stake. The sick and the frail expect their cure, in the end, from his mere passing by, from a word of his. The terror of the crucifixion is expressed in the faces of the disciples and the women. And in the Emmaus picture we read in the features of the disciples the amazing truth: *Christ lives*!

Georg Simmel notes that at the first glance Rembrandt's Christ looks more insignificant than the people around him: 'And yet, if we look just a little longer, that weak, almost faltering being becomes the only really firm one, and all the other strong and substantial figures are uncertain and almost uprooted beside him, as if he alone, not they, were standing on the ground on which man can truly stand.'[10]

What then distinguishes this man from the others? He is not less human, nor is he a superman, a hero. But his words and his deeds decide. According to the Scriptures: 'The multitudes were astonished at his teaching, for he taught them as one having authority.'[11]

Between 1648 and 1661 Rembrandt painted 'portraits of Christ' no less than eleven times, that is to say, paintings which represent the head of Christ alone. Does this mean, as has been suggested, that he had at that time a particularly suitable model for this purpose? Probably yes, for the features on all these paintings are very similar indeed and we can add the 'King David' of 1651 (Br 611). But, as is so often the case in Rembrandt's work, the model is only a point of departure and there can be no doubt that the painter goes much further than a mere realistic portrayal of his model. He is obviously seeking to present Christ as he has come to see him inwardly. It is worth noting that there is good reason to infer that these are not painted at the request of others, for the inventory of 1656 mentions two 'heads of Christ'.

At first sight these representations of Christ seem extremely traditional. Has Rembrandt been under the indirect influence of the mediaeval legend of Lentulus? Many details of the description of Christ's features given in that legend can be found in Rembrandt's paintings, such as the waving hair, the parting in the middle 'after the manner of the Nazarenes', and the abundant but short beard. And yet it is practically impossible to find in the history of art any precedent for this representation of Christ. There has been nothing quite like it. This is not the majestic Christ of the Byzantines or of Michelangelo, not the Christ who is above all to be pitied as in so much mediaeval art or in the art of Guido Reni; nor the classic youth of the Renaissance painters, nor the hero of the art of the Counter-Reformation. This is a very human Christ, and yet we can see for ourselves (and it is proved by the close relation of this series with the 'Emmaus' of 1648 and by the fact that one of these eleven is clearly a 'Christ after the Resurrection') that this is the Saviour and the Son of God. Each of these gives a specific accent: the praying Christ (Br 623 and 625); the Christ who bears the sins of the world (Br 621, 624, 627); the Christ who forgives (Br 626); the Christ who reveals the divine mysteries (Br 629); and the Risen Christ (Br 630). In each case however we have to do with Christ who has come to be with and among men, who is meek and lowly of heart and who with his divine authority calls to himself all who are weary and burdened.

As Rembrandt deeply understood the mystery of the Incarnation he was able in the passion story to express the whole tension contained in the gospel between God's wrath and his mercy. Some painters have represented the crucifixion more eloquently. But their very eloquence is suspect. Rembrandt does not omit anything of the biblical story. In the second version of the *Three Crosses* we feel all the human and cosmic horror of Golgotha. But he does not add anything either; for we cannot add anything where 'all things are accomplished'. In the repeated interpretations of Gethsemane Rembrandt's message finds its strongest expression. This theme, which is so rare in his earlier works, is treated again and again between 1650 and 1660 (etching of 1652, as well as a series of six drawings, all

of the same time). The last and hardest struggle of
Christ quite fills the thoughts of the painter, and he
achieves an extreme simplification of style without a
single superfluous stroke. Everything is reduced, concentrated, condensed to the last possible element.
This element is the struggle of the Son of God who is
forsaken and at the same time supported by God.
Luther and several old Dutch editions of the Bible
translate Luke 22.44 as follows: 'And it came about that
he struggled with death.' Rembrandt represents the
main stages of that struggle: the prayer 'Not my will,
but thine, be done' (Drawing: Valentiner 451),* an
angel strengthening him (etching and drawings 452, 453
and 454),* the return to the sleeping disciples (drawings 449 and 450).* Everywhere there is the same sad-
ness 'unto death', for, deserted by all, Jesus bears the
burden of the sins of all mankind. The complete loneliness of Christ is stressed by the indifference and lack
of understanding on the part of the disciples. The
etching furthermore expresses the cosmic importance
of the event: the whole of nature is included in that
struggle on which the fate of the world depends. But
at the moment when the hostile powers threaten to
crush Jesus, God intervenes. The presence of the angel
reveals to us the ultimate meaning of the gospel:
God's last word is not judgment and death, but mercy
and life.

The opinion has been expressed that this spiritually
tempted and almost broken Christ as represented by
Rembrandt must have seemed almost blasphemous to
the Lutheran and Reformed orthodoxy of the seventeenth century, and that such a picture of Christ was
much more likely to have grown out of Mennonite

ideas.[12] But anyone who takes the trouble to read the
poetry of Rembrandt's time, especially that written by
people near to him, will realize that this opinion is
untenable.[13] Both Jeremias de Decker, Rembrandt's
friend, and Heiman Dullaert, his pupil, who were
good Reformed believers, have spoken in their poems,
with stirring words, of Christ's spiritual suffering and
total dereliction, and of the mystery of the divine
incognito. In his *Christus in 't Hofken* Dullaert asks:

Heeft u Gods toorn een pijl in 't ingewand gezonen
Die uw beangst gemoed zoo vinnig praamt en wringt?

Has God's wrath sent an arrow into you,
Which so sharply pierces your soul in its agony?

In his *Good Friday*, Decker describes how Christ 'is
almost devoured by the tortures of hell', and then he
puts into words what we have seen is the core of
Rembrandt's understanding of the gospel:

De bange mist ('t is waer) der menschelijke qualen
Houdt hier een wijl de stralen
Van syne Godtheijd doof:
Maar waert ghij niet verblind door nijd en ongeloof,
Ghij soud in hem iet meer als menschelijks sien stralen
Ook door de mist der qualen.

The cloudy mist, it is true, of human torment
For a time dulls the rays
Of his divinity,
But if you were not blind through envy or lack of faith,
You would see more shine forth from him than human
*   frailty,*
Even through the mist of torment.

This does not necessarily mean that Rembrandt

learned these things from his Reformed brethren. It is quite possible that he discovered them for himself in his Bible. But it does mean that there were people near him, Reformed and perhaps others too, who understood the same dimension of the gospel.

Since Rembrandt represented Christ in such a purely human way, some people see in him an advocate of pure humanism. According to them, his Christ is not the Son of God, the Saviour, but simply the preacher of love, the Jesus in the sense of Ernest Renan. This is a profound misunderstanding. If we remember the central place which is given to the cross in Rembrandt's work, we understand that there he sees the heart of history, and the decisive event of universal meaning. Hans Martin Rotermund has made an interesting remark, in an essay, about the importance of the rays in Rembrandt's biblical pictures:[14] he shows that the rays which surround Christ's head in some of Rembrandt's drawings must not be interpreted as a stereotyped halo, but as the sign by which Christ is recognized as God's son. There are drawings of Christ meeting the disciples on their way to Emmaus, where these rays are missing because the disciples have not yet recognized him. But there are others representing the moment of the breaking of the bread and of the recognition, where the rays stress the fact of this recognition. On the other hand, some drawings of the meeting between Christ and men indicate by single rays the moment when Christ is recognized as the Lord and Messiah. The plainness of these examples leaves no doubt that thus Rembrandt wanted to express that in the last resort it is the knowledge of faith which counts. Similarly the rays (which can also be seen in the Gethsemane pictures of this book) mean that Christ receives help from his Father. We may be certain, then, that for Rembrandt Christ was not only the prophetic preacher, but the Messiah and the Mediator. I think it is important to note that the drawings in which the rays have that special significance practically all date from the time after 1642, when Rembrandt no longer uses the Bible, but interprets it.[15]

Rotermund is right in saying that this symbol of the rays expresses the very personal relation of the believer to the figure of Christ. But he is wrong in remarking that such a personal relation with Christ is unlikely within the Reformed Church. In the writings of Voetius, in the poems of Dullaert, Revius and de Decker, we find clear proofs of such a personal relation. Some of their poems have been written in the form of a conversation between Christ and the poet. The famous sonnet of the theologian Revius may serve as an example. The first line runs as follows:

> *T'en zijn de Joden niet, Heer Jesu, die U kruisten*
> *It was not the Jews, Lord Jesus, who crucified you*

and further on he confesses:

> *Ik ben't, o Heer, ik ben't die U dit heb gedaan.*
> *It is I, O Lord, it is I who have done that to you.*

CHAPTER FOUR

The Virgin Mary
in Rembrandt's Work

* * *

IF the Bible is the main source of Rembrandt's religious inspiration, as we have just seen, how is it with the themes derived from Roman Catholic iconography, and what is the artist's attitude towards the theological questions raised by traditional art? This problem deserves special treatment.

Although the religious themes borrowed from tradition are a minority in Rembrandt's work, they are there all the same, for the master has not always been the revolutionary innovator some people have seen in him. He knows the classic art of painting by heart.[1] How does he make use of it?

The representations of the Virgin Mary, and especially the etchings and drawings of which she is the central figure, may help us to know Rembrandt's attitude in this question.

First we may note that most of those representations of the Virgin date from Rembrandt's 'baroque' period (1630 to 1642). It is all the more interesting to see how he translates that baroque style into his own language. And we realize that, while accepting the influence of the style of that school, he gives his own religious interpretation.

A drawing of 1635 presents a Virgin directly

modelled upon Raphael's *Madonna della Sedia*.[2] We notice a surprising change, however. In the place of the young woman who was endowed by Raphael with all the charms of her beauty, but who was painted with a face devoid of any expression, Rembrandt shows a Mary in the same general posture, but whose faraway look is lost in sad thought. Out of a carefree Madonna without mystery he has made a mother who 'ponders all these things in her heart'.

The *Death of Mary* (etching of 1639) also belongs to the baroque period in style, and hints of earlier representations can easily be detected here too. But again, Rembrandt's conception of the theme gives it a completely new content, and a stamp of his own.

According to tradition, the Virgin was expected to lie in state as on a throne, surrounded by apostles who sing her praise. Roman Catholic theologians even asserted that she left the world without suffering.[3] So the whole stress was laid on the glorious homecoming of the Mother of God. Even Dürer's picture is imbued with an atmosphere of pious glorification.

Now at first glance it seems as if Rembrandt, like the artists of the Counter-Reformation, wanted to represent Mary's death as a pompous ecclesiastical ceremony. The bed of state, the high priest, the pathetic gestures of the apostle St John and of the woman beside him, the angels, all carried out in dynamic baroque style, at first give us the impression that here we are faced with a Rembrandt who has quite succumbed to the current iconographic fashion. Weisbach is not altogether wrong when he speaks of 'a kind of baroque blood and thunder with heavenly assistance'.[4] But on a closer look we realize that the event in the centre of the etching is in no way meant to be pompous and ceremonious. On the contrary: Mary dying in complete self-surrender, and Peter, who so much wants to help her, and the matter-of-fact doctor, all these are taking part not in a public representative event, but in a very simple human one—the death of a beloved mother. This part of the etching is not pageantry, it is the farewell a human being takes of those with whom she has lived in true fellowship. Here we see Rembrandt at the cross-roads. Two voices are speaking at the same time, the loud voice of baroque style, and the quiet voice of the Bible. It is promising indeed that he listens to the quiet voice where the essential thing is concerned. Only later did he find an entirely adequate expression for this voice.

Further there is an etching of 1641 which, seen formally, takes up again the iconographic theme of the glorification of Mary.[5] The Virgin is being carried along by clouds.* Here too Rembrandt was influenced by an Italian model. In his inventory we find engravings by Federigo Barocci (No. 195). Barocci is a typical representative of baroque piety, indeed 'one of the artists who helped in fashioning the specific outlook of the Counter-Reformation'.[6] His engraving, *Virgin and Child seated on the Clouds* is a glorification which represents Mary as an amiable and handsome young woman with the child. Rembrandt takes the composition over, but does not merely copy it for he transforms it completely. The angelic Madonna of Barocci has changed into a human mother who knows even now that 'a sword shall pierce through her own soul'. The glorified Madonna has changed into 'a sorrowful Mary', as the early description of the etching

44

shows.[7] The halo which as a matter of course crowns Barocci's Mary, has become a garland of light surrounding the whole picture. But Rembrandt stresses the fact that salvation is brought by the child, and not by Mary, by letting a special radiance shine from the child. This sorrowful Mary should really be on earth, and not in the clouds. Once again, this etching gives proof of the inner tension in which Rembrandt lived in those years. Content and form, intention and expression are conflicting with one another.

A drawing of about 1633 unexpectedly confirms this impression.[8] On the side of several studies for a *Mater Dolorosa* Rembrandt has scribbled some words which may be translated as follows: 'Pious obedience (*dyvoot tgheehoor*) kept in her pure heart as a comfort for her trembling soul.' Anyone who is ignorant of the Reformers and, like Emile Mâle, thinks that 'Luther and Calvin tried to wipe out from the memory of men that wonderful figure (the virgin) which had been shaped nearer to perfection by each century',[9] may consider that those words of Rembrandt contain very little Protestantism. But anyone who has read Luther's *Magnificat* or Calvin's commentaries on the first chapter of St Luke's Gospel, finds here a true echo of the texts. Luther presents Mary as the greatest pattern of true humility, as one who expects everything from God. She proclaims undeserved grace, Luther says, and her message is so precious that we must take care not to let it be suffocated by the cult of Mary, for 'the more we attribute deserving merit to her, the more we take away from divine grace and lessen the truth of the Magnificat'.[10] And Calvin adds: 'God has looked upon her, however disregarded and despised she was. From which follows that all those are false honours and not due to Mary, which do not solely praise God's omnipotence and undeserved kindness.'[11]

There is a certain indirect attack upon the celestial idealized Madonnas of tradition in Rembrandt's pictures of Mary, and especially in his almost brutal way of stressing the Virgin's lowliness.[12] We are reminded of Luther's other remark: 'The masters who so depict and shape the Blessed Virgin for us as to leave nothing despised in her, but only high things,— what do they do but confront us with her alone, and not her along with God?'[13]

It is not very likely that Rembrandt read Luther's or Calvin's writings, but their spirit, which lives in the Protestant translations of the Bible, made a deep and lasting impression on him. In the Vulgate, Mary praises the Lord who has regarded her humility, and the traditional interpretation speaks of Mary's humble *attitude*. Luther and Calvin however gave different translations, based on the relevant texts of the Old Testament, because they knew that only he is truly humble who is not aware of his own humility. Their translations say that Mary praises the Lord because he has regarded the low estate of his handmaid. This interpretation can be found even in the old Dutch translations and was taken over into the synodal version of 1637.[14]

This way we better understand the gulf which separates Rembrandt's *ancilla domini* from the *regina coeli* of the Roman Catholic liturgy, this 'king's daughter desired for her beauty's sake', who in Roman Catholic theology is declared 'far more beautiful not only than the daughters of men, but also than the angels'.[15] Certainly Emile Mâle is right in maintaining that the innovators take away from the Virgin all beauty, all poetry, all greatness, for this is exactly what Luther has done in theology, and Rembrandt in religious painting. But he is wrong in insinuating that they did so with the intention 'of robbing Christendom of the Virgin'. On the contrary, the Virgin was dear to those 'innovators', because she was the visible proof that 'God hath chosen things which are not, to bring to nought things that are'.

It has been asserted that Rembrandt's love of the figure of Mary does not spring from the spirit of the Reformed Church, but corresponds to the attitude of the Mennonites towards the Mother of Jesus.[16] To assert this, betrays ignorance of Christian poetry in the Holland of the seventeenth century. Jacobus Revius, Professor in the Theological Faculty of Leyden, one of the collaborators in the synodal translation of the Bible, wrote moving poems about Mary. The following lines by Revius sound like an echo of the words of Rembrandt we have just heard:

Maer salich boven al sijn sulcke die haer leven
(Gelijck Maria dee) tot sijnen dienst begeven
En hebben in sijn woort haer hertelijcke lust[17]

But blessed before all are those who devote their lives,
As Mary did, to his service,
And truly rejoice in his word.

The testimony of the Reformed poet Jeremias de Decker is even more important, for he was in close touch with Rembrandt and the only Dutch poet of importance who in his poems speaks of Rembrandt's art with deep understanding. There are lines in his

Good Friday, which must have been known to Rembrandt:[18]

> *Hij siet sijn 'moeder hier met half gebroken 'oogen*
> *Tot in haer siel bewogen*
> *Om 't geen hij uyt moet staen,*
> *Ja door haer' droeve siel een swaerd van droefheyd gaen'*

> *He sees his mother here with half-broken eyes,*
> *Moved to the depths of her soul*
> *By what he has to endure,*
> *A sword of sadness pierces her sorrowful soul.*

CHAPTER FIVE

The Miracle of Christmas

★   ★   ★

A MONG the great artists Rembrandt is one of the few who in their representation of the Christmas story have expressed the whole paradoxical harshness of the Incarnation. The great majority of painters do not allow the gospel to speak for itself, but make of the Christmas story either a poetic legend acted in celestial spheres, or else quite a worldly event. Few of them have grasped the importance of accepting the mystery of the birth of God's son without giving it a purely divine or purely earthly interpretation.

Rembrandt too, certainly did not grasp the import of this message from the beginning. In his youth, he portrayed the *Angel Appearing to the Shepherds* as an amazing natural miracle (etching of 1634); or he made of the *Holy Family*, the ideal model of a happy earthly family (painting of 1631, Munich). But from 1642 on, he gradually began to discover in tranquil contemplation the deeper significance of Christ's birth. He knows that Bethlehem means that God himself intervenes and that this can only be comprehended by faith. As in all his religious painting, he abandons here too everything external which might attract the eye, everything majestic and angelic, so that the reality of the event, its concrete and human character, can no

49

longer be doubted. The most important thing, however, is not what can be seen, as he emphasizes explicitly. It is the fact that this weak child in the manger is the Saviour of the world.

Some examples may help us to understand Rembrandt's Christmas message better. We choose *Adoration of the Shepherds,** *Adoration of the Magi** and *Joseph's Dream.**

Adoration of the Shepherds

This etching,[1] finished in 1654 and generally known under the title *Adoration of the Shepherds with the Lamp*, probably strikes many people as quite an ordinary picture. But might not this very ordinariness conceal the message of the artist? The Bible does not tell us that Jesus was born in a classical ruin (as the artists of the Renaissance from Mantegna to Veronese represent it); it does not say that Mary was dressed in a gorgeous garment, nor that the shepherds were picturesque figures in an Arcadian play (as they are in the pictures of Coreggio and many others). The Madonna of the Counter-Reformation who in joy and pride tries to direct the observer's eye to her child is not known to the Bible. How much simpler and plainer is Scripture. Anyone who tries to say more than it does, says less.

Goethe defended Rembrandt against those who say, 'The Italians did that better'. He said 'Cold refinement and the stiff ecclesiastical propriety have caused all the biblical passages to be pulled out of their simplicity and truth and torn away from the sympathizing heart, in order to dazzle the gaping eyes of dullness. Do Mary and the boy not sit before the shepherds, among the ornaments of all the altar frames, as if they were on show for money, or as if she had prepared for the honour of this visit after four weeks' rest with all the leisure of childbed and the joys of womanhood?'[2]

Here now we see quite an ordinary shed. Father is sitting on a wheelbarrow, mother on the straw. Shepherds are arriving with their wives and children. One has brought his bagpipe along. A small boy is gazing at the newly born child with great interest. Could there be a more human, a more ordinary scene?

And yet something extraordinary seems to be happening in this scene and giving it a deeper meaning. The attitude of the shepherds indicates that they have just discovered something tremendous. It is not the quite natural neighbourly curiosity at the birth of a child. Their joy is mingled with awe and amazement. The shepherd who is taking off his hat has suddenly seen a great light, and another lifts his hands as if for prayer.

A handful of men have grasped the certainty and the truth contained in this incredible message of a saviour 'wrapped in swaddling-clothes and laid in a manger'. Joseph seems to say: 'I do not understand it either, but it is so: this child is the Messiah promised by God.' And his mother? She is not sitting on a throne, she does not dream of parading her child before the spectators. Her gaze is lost in the distance. Her joy is overshadowed by the grief which she foresees in the fate of her son.

The Adoration of the Magi

At first sight the painting of the year 1657 representing the *Adoration of the Magi** (Buckingham Palace), seems to be influenced much more strongly by tradition. There are a number of details here borrowed by Rembrandt from the works of painters known to him. A comparison of this picture with an earlier work on the same theme (Gothenburg Museum 1630), or with contemporary works, shows, however, that Rembrandt has learnt something new.

In his early work, and in practically all contemporary representations of the Adoration of the Magi, the romantic contents of the subject has tempted the artists: the pomp of the magnificent pageant dominates their works completely. At least Christ and the three magi are encompassed by the brilliance of earthly splendour. Think of, say, the paintings by Gentile da Fabriano or Benozzo Gozzoli in Florence, where the splendour of the wise men plays such a prominent part that we forget why in fact they came to Bethlehem; or the paintings by Rubens in Antwerp and the Louvre, where the adoration of the child forms the central part of the picture, the atmosphere is full of the joy of a solemn religious festival, rather than that which fills men when they meet their Messiah for the first time.

The mature Rembrandt offers us quite a different thing. The wise men are certainly kings, but their royal dignity vanishes when they meet the divine child. So the old king who is kneeling before the child has given his crown to a companion. He is now nothing but a simple human being who has found his Lord and Saviour. The second king is handing his crown to a page whom at the same time he pushes back, lest the devout silence be disturbed by him. The third king is just discovering his true Saviour in the child and is shrinking back with astonishment. They have really understood the mystery of the birth of Christ. The beauty of the mother and the child are of no more importance. For when God acts, the voices of this world are silenced.

And Mary? She is the humble servant who suffers God's great work to be fulfilled in her, and looks at her own child full of astonishment and adoration. She does not try to push herself forward. God's deeds need no advertisement, they speak for themselves.

Joseph's Dream

The third picture, *Joseph's Dream*,* of 1645 (Kaiser-Friedrich Museum, Berlin) perhaps shows most clearly Rembrandt's susceptibility for the dramatic contents of the Christmas story. All those who see the summit of Christian art in Raphael and in the hey-day of the Renaissance will find in this picture the ultimate proof of Rembrandt approaching the mystery of Christ's birth without any veneration. According to them, as to Jacob Burckhardt, 'the Holy, if it is to have an effect as such, absolutely demands at least purified and inoffensive forms',[3] and they cannot bear that 'enormous ugliness of forms'—Rembrandt's forms. Certainly we must not look for types of human beauty in that peasant woman, in that sleeping tramp. They have nothing in common with the St Joseph of Roman Catholic art, 'that angelic figure endowed with all excellent qualities'.[4] Here Joseph is a very ordinary and almost helpless human being who is carried away with the stream of events overwhelming him. There is something deliberately offensive in this curt realism. But does the Bible assert that God's son lived on this earth in such a way that he did not give 'offence'? No, it certainly says the contrary. The world did not apprehend the light because it was a hidden one. And the parents who found no room at the inn and had to flee to Egypt by night are witnesses that God 'exalts him that humbles himself', and that he chose 'the base things of the world, and the things that are despised'.

It is that unbelievable relation between God's mercy and man's misery which Rembrandt meant to express in his painting. Joseph and Mary fulfil no other purpose in their human existence than that of obeying God; they cannot defend themselves against a world which denies their child a place. But a light shines in the darkness of their distress. Once again God acts and looks 'upon their low estate'.

There is help, because there is a Saviour. The angel is bending over Joseph as God's mercy bends over a man's life. And Mary can join in the praise: 'And his mercy is unto generations and generations of them that fear him.'

Sometimes Rembrandt's Christmas message seems to be severe and harsh. There is no picture, from his maturer years at least, which transforms Christmas into a touching idyll. He sees the shadow of the cross over the manger. But the way in which he proclaims the joy of Christmas, deepens its content all the more. The joy he knows of does not depend on any earthly conditions; it springs from the one fact that a Saviour has been born to us, which is Christ the Lord.

CHAPTER SIX

A Sermon:
The Hundred Guilder Print

★ ★ ★

THE *Hundred Guilder Print** belongs to a group of
paintings, etchings and drawings which were
made after 1645, that is, at a time when Rembrandt gained a new and deepened understanding of the
gospel.

This etching may not be one of the most profound
pictures created by Rembrandt in those decisive years.
Works like *Three Crosses* and *Christ Teaching* speak even
more distinctly to us, for there the artist's whole
creative power is concentrated on one single theme.
But all the same this great etching contains valuable
evidence for a better understanding of Rembrandt as
an exegete.

The official name of the etching, *Jesus Healing the
Sick,* is no more correct than its popular one, *The
Hundred Guilder Print*. In reality it should be called
St Matthew 19,[1] for Rembrandt has clearly tried to
present to us the contents of the whole of that chapter.
Let us see how he interprets the text.

'And great multitudes followed him; and he healed
them there.' It is as though a stream of human misery
were emerging from a dark cave. Sick and frail people
are groping for the way that is to take them to the
light. (Note the right-hand side of the picture where all
the lines run towards Jesus.) What can we say about

those people? Their whole existence is one cry for help and salvation. In themselves, they are nothing and have nothing: they expect everything from the Lord who is standing in their midst. Social differences disappear before him. (Beggars are standing beside well-dressed women.)

Here the skill of the physician is of no more avail; one single hope remains: a miracle wrought by God. It is that miracle which they all expect. Can anyone pray more fervently than the woman who is looking up to Jesus with her hands clasped? And what does the groping hand of the blind woman on the pallet mean but the groping for true salvation?

'And there came unto him Pharisees, tempting him, and saying, "Is it lawful for a man to put away his wife for every cause?" And he answered . . .' Of that discussion our picture only shows the result: The indignation of the Pharisees about the shocking assertions of this Jesus. He has spoken of their hardness of heart, and what is much worse, he has placed himself above Moses in saying: '*And I say unto you.*' On the left side of the picture we see the Pharisees unanimously rejecting this heresy, this blasphemy. They deliberately turn away from Jesus. One of them is smiling ironically, another is looking indignant. They are beginning to ask themselves how they can get rid of this troublesome fellow.

'Then were there brought unto him little children, that he should lay his hands on them, and pray: and the disciples rebuked them. But Jesus said, Suffer the little children to come unto me, and forbid them not: for of such is the kingdom of heaven.' One woman is bringing her child. A small boy with an impatient gesture is pulling his hesitant mother by her skirt towards Christ. Peter is about to intervene, for the Lord has other things to do. But he blesses them. Why does he do so? The answer is given in the spontaneous, trusting action of the boy. He does it, because the children follow the call of the Messiah so simply, so unconditionally, because they go to him full of expectations, just like the sick.

'And behold, one came to him and said, Master, what good thing shall I do? . . . Jesus said unto him, . . . go, sell that thou hast. . . . But when the young man heard the saying, he went away sorrowful.' It is the rich young man. His chin cupped in his hand, depressed, he is sitting before Jesus in his beautiful garments, a living example of the appalling poverty of the rich. He is a prisoner of his many possessions and cannot give himself up to Christ. While the children are not yet bound to this world, and while the sick are no more bound to it, this young man is its slave.

There is another who cannot move, nor does he try: it is the big, fat man in the left-hand corner in front. St Matthew does not mention him. What is he doing here? Is he meant to fill a gap? No, it is enough to look at him somewhat more closely, and we understand that he represents the eternal looker-on, the only one who is neutral. It is amazing how a broad back, two hands grasping a stick, two feet which seem to be screwed to the ground, can be so laden with eloquence, can express so much indifference and petty-bourgeois self-sufficiency. Nothing moves that man, who is so comfortable on this earth. He is smiling about all the excitement around him. If we could find a name for him, it might be Pilate.

But what is all this for? Can this print really be called a sermon? Have we not rather to do with a subtle but useless play with biblical motives? We shall find the answer only on returning to the centre of the print? Not much can be said of Rembrandt's Christ. We cannot possibly claim that he corresponds to a certain type, that he is specially sublime, of great kindness, or very heroic. All these trivial expressions seem absurd if applied to the importance of this man. The only special thing about him is that he is standing in the centre; everything that happens has its beginning, its meaning and its end in *him*. It is he who sends out a call and who demands an answer. Some are going towards him (sick people and children), others are struggling away from him (the Pharisees and the rich young man), like the ebb and flow of the tide. He who thinks he can play the spectator will invariably be pulled away from him. Christ is the key-figure. But neither his looks, nor his words, nor his action invite people to recognize in him their Saviour. 'Neither shall any one hear his voice in the streets' (Matt. 12.19). There he is standing without any 'visible difference' (Pascal), without any obvious confirmation of what he is. This Christ is predestined to be 'set for the falling and rising up of many in Israel; and for a sign which is spoken against' (Luke 2.34). There is demanded the clear decision to recognize in this man the true Messiah. God wants men to *believe* in him. Hence his ambassador does not come down to the earth in heavenly form, but in the shape of a man, a simple and suffering man, devoid of beauty. Blessed is he to whom he is not a stumbling-block.

So Rembrandt does not at all feel it his duty to

persuade the spectator, and to prove to him that the sick and the children are right, and the Pharisees wrong. He only wants to make his confession. By placing Christ in the centre he shows that there are people who have heard the call of the Saviour and received his gift of divine grace. The painter's language remains *indirect*. But did not Jesus himself thus speak of himself when to the messengers of John the Baptist he gave the veiled answer: 'Go your way and tell John the things which ye do hear and see'?

So we discover Rembrandt's true way of 'preaching', which finds its expression not only in the *Hundred Guilder Print*, but in all the biblical work of his maturity. In a century when propaganda replaced witness, when Christian art was mainly concerned with proving Christ's divine nature by outward signs, Rembrandt dared to make Christ speak for himself. He knew that we must not try to know more than God who sent us his son in the shape of a servant. He could hardly know the thesis Martin Luther had advanced at Heidelberg; but in reading the Bible he reached the same conclusion: 'So that it is not enough nor does it help anybody to recognize God in his honour and majesty, unless he recognizes him in the lowliness and shame of the cross.' He knew that our salvation depends on what we believe and not on what we see. Therefore he, the seer, to whom seeing must have been a temptation, denied himself the painting of an obvious and glorified Christ. His Christ is never without the shadow of the cross. It is this which makes Rembrandt a biblical artist, and thus a true master of exegesis.

CHAPTER SEVEN

Rembrandt and the Church

★ ★ ★

WE have no direct information either from Rembrandt himself or from those who knew him personally about his attitude to the Church. But we have on the one hand the documents of the church archives and on the other a statement of the Italian Baldinucci based on data supplied by a Danish pupil of Rembrandt's. Now the great difficulty is that the archives seem to prove clearly that Rembrandt belonged to the Reformed Church, but that according to Baldinucci Rembrandt was, at least in the forties, a Mennonite.

The question is of course whether we can take Baldinucci's remark seriously. He was never in Holland and his information was, moreover, second-hand, from a Dane who may not quite have understood the Dutch situation. It is remarkable, though, that Baldinucci, when speaking of the Mennonites, uses the typically Dutch word 'Menist',[1] and describes the main points of their creed fairly correctly, and that he gives us a lively report of other aspects of Rembrandt's life. So we cannot disregard his opinion.

We now must examine both possibilities: Was Rembrandt of the Reformed or the Mennonite community? It would be senseless to ask further whether he belonged to yet another church or group. Since Neumann's book about Rembrandt appeared, much has been written about Rembrandt's possible relations to the Collegiants (a group which sought to return to a simplified form of Christianity without elaborate doctrine and without external organization), the Socinians and mystical groups connected with Boehme. There is no reason at all why we should see a connection between Rembrandt and any of those groups. Nothing indicates that he was connected with the leaders of the Collegiants[2] (Adam Boreel, Galenus) or with the Socinians, nor do we know whether he ever heard of Spinoza and Descartes, both of whom lived in Amsterdam at the same time as Rembrandt.

It is misleading to draw conclusions about the artist's point of view from the fact that he knew men who were somehow connected with adherents of one *Weltanschauung* or another, or that he lived in a town where there was a group upholding such and such a view—especially in the Amsterdam of the seventeenth century, where all sorts of sects, groups and circles with different views of life were vying with one another. Our examination of possible influences on Rembrandt should be confined to *direct* and *lasting* connection only. So we can leave aside the question of possible relations with Collegiants, Socinians and groups associated with Boehme's mysticism, as long as we have no proof that Rembrandt was in direct and lasting connection with the leaders of such groups.

We shall proceed chronologically and examine the documents of the twenties and thirties which are quite unambiguous in their language. Rembrandt's parents were married in the Reformed Church. It is therefore quite certain that Rembrandt was brought up in the Reformed faith. But before long he came into contact with Mennonites. In 1631 he went to live in the house of Hendrick Uylenburch in Amsterdam; he belonged to a branch of the Uylenburch family which had joined the Mennonites. It is probable that during this period Rembrandt came to know other members of the Mennonite community. But there is not the slightest reason to think that he changed his own confession. On the contrary—his own marriage with Saskia van Uylenburch took place in the Reformed Church. Now it had been decreed by the Synod of Dordrecht (1618-19) that persons who 'were completely estranged from the Reformed Church'[3] were not allowed to be publicly married in a Reformed congregation. More-over Rembrandt's wife, Saskia van Uylenburch, came from a strict Reformed family. During the period of her engagement, Saskia stayed with her sister Antje, who during that time fell ill and died.[4] This sister was married to the Professor of Theology, Johannes Maccovius, who had immigrated to Holland from Poland.

This Maccovius played a remarkable part in the theological and ecclesiastical life of the seventeenth century.[5] He was an extremely able theologian who attempted to make the old scholastic forms of thought fruitful for Calvinist dogmatics, and pursued this attempt to its utmost consequences. He was notori-ously aggressive and a specialist in theological pole-mics. His life was a series of theological squabbles. He was also accused of having indulged in wild orgies with his students in Franeker. But not all those accusations (especially of the year 1626) must be accepted as true, for in that case, the van Uylenburch family would not have sanctioned his marriage with Antje which took place in the same year.

The discussions of the Synod of Dordrecht make it especially evident that Maccovius was a very extreme Calvinist. At the Synod he was charged with having drawn far too extreme conclusions from the doctrine of predestination in his scholastic argumentation; with having taught, for instance, that sin had been willed by God.[6] The Synod declared that Maccovius had not proclaimed any heresy, but that henceforth he should be more careful in his manner of expression in order not to give offence.

This redoubtable polemicist was, of course, also an opponent of the Mennonites, and wrote against them particularly.[7] Everything we know of this theologian indicates that he would not have admitted Saskia into his house had she been engaged to a Mennonite.

From approximately 1633 Rembrandt was also on friendly terms with the Reformed minister Sylvius, a cousin of Saskia, and with his family. Sylvius acted on Saskia's behalf at the registration of her marriage, was a godfather at the baptism of their first child in 1635, and himself baptized a daughter of Rembrandt and Saskia in 1638, shortly before his death.[8] Rembrandt had also etched Sylvius's portrait in 1634, the year of his marriage.[9] At the family's request he made a painting of the deceased minister in 1644 (or 1645),[10] and an etching in 1646.[11] Rembrandt must have preserved a strong personal impression of Sylvius to enable him to give such a living representation of him eight years after his death. But surely Sylvius would not have welcomed Rembrandt so kindly into his family if Rembrandt had been a Mennonite.

Of further importance are the four documents of the years 1635, 1638, 1640 and 1641,[12] about the baptism of Rembrandt's and Saskia's children. All four name the father and mother and also the godparents (these always from among Saskia's relations). During a baptism in the Reformed Church the parents had to answer very precise questions. Thus they were asked: 'Do you confess to the doctrine as it is contained in the Old and New Testaments and in the articles of the Christian faith, and taught in this Christian church here, as being the true and perfect doctrine of salvation?' For a Mennonite not only the fact of infant baptism but also an affirmative reply to this question were impossible.

It has been pointed out several times that Rembrandt's style of living at this time did not fit in with the 'ultra-puritan manners' of the Mennonites.[13] It is however quite possible that he continued to meet a number of Mennonites. Commissions arrived from various quarters, presumably also from Mennonites, as recent investigations have indicated. The artist maintained friendly relations with people of very different church loyalties at that time. So he painted the great leader of the Remonstrants, Uytenbogaerdt,[14] in 1633 (and an etching in 1635);[15] but in 1637 Rembrandt was engaged in painting the portrait of the Reformed minister Eleasar Swalmius,[16] who had just played a leading part in the struggle against the Remonstrants.[17]

So it is unlikely that Rembrandt had very close relations with the Mennonites in the twenties and thirties. But what about the forties? Baldinucci's information becomes important here; not only because he tells us quite plainly that he is speaking of the time around 1640 but also because his authority, Bernhard Keihl, was Rembrandt's pupil from 1642 to 1644.[18]

In the year 1640 Rembrandt made a drawing of the Mennonite preacher Claesz Anslo.[19] In 1641, he etched Anslo,[20] and in the same year he painted Anslo together with his wife.[21] The care given to the preparation of those pictures, and especially the successful attempt to characterize Anslo as a pastor, give us the impression that Rembrandt and Anslo were friends. Since Baldinucci's note about Rembrandt's Mennonite inclinations is based on information of the years 1642 to 1644, it is at any rate possible that at that period Rembrandt had drawn nearer to the Mennonites, and that Anslo served as the mediator. Now Anslo belonged to the 'Waterlanders', one of the many subdivisions of the Mennonites, who in common with other Mennonites cultivated the ideal of the 'pure community' and maintained the necessity of excommunication as a means of realizing the Church 'without blemish or wrinkle', but who, in the handling of church discipline, avoided rigorism.[22] Within his congregation Anslo advocated the orthodox teaching of the Mennonite confessions. So he opposed those who, about 1622, tried to spread Socinian (i.e. anti-trinitarian) doctrines among the Waterlanders. It is probable, therefore, that Rembrandt got to know Mennonitism in its evangelical form, and not in its more rationalistic form.[23] Must we suppose then that Baldinucci's information is correct? Certainly not in the way he formulated it. He said Rembrandt professed (*professava*) the 'religion' of the 'Menisti'. That would mean that he had joined a Mennonite congregation.

This is unlikely because we should then have heard more about such an important step either from the Reformed, or from the Mennonite side; and also because the sad story of his relations with Geertghe Dircx, the 'illicit' union with Hendrickje, and the bankruptcy, would inevitably have led to Rembrandt's expulsion from the Mennonite community.

But it is not impossible that at that time Rembrandt was in close touch with the Mennonites. The early forties brought about a great change in his life. The *Night Watch* meant a self-revival in his art, Saskia's death meant loneliness. He may have wondered at that time if he could find spiritual help among the Mennonites, and he may have gone to their services. This would then explain why Keihl in Rome spoke of his relations to the Mennonites, and why Baldinucci said Rembrandt was a Mennonite 'at that time', and that he did not know 'whether Rembrandt had remained in that false religion'.

If this is so, Rembrandt may have been stimulated by Mennonite ideas and life.[24] But Rotermund goes too far when he says that his 'existence as a Christian was formed by it'.[25] This would be correct only if it could be proved that themes and views were wrought into his work which he could *only* find with the Mennonites. But this is not so. For all the so-called typically Mennonite elements which have been mentioned as examples Rembrandt might just as well have been drawn from his personal intercourse with the Bible or, as we have already said, from Reformed circles.

As for the fifties, in 1651 Rembrandt painted the portrait of the Reformed minister Eleazar Swalmius for the second time. The picture itself is lost, but the rhymes of the minister Geldorpius on the engraving by J. Suyderhoef (document No. 132) prove that Rembrandt painted Swalmius in that year. This seems to indicate that up to that period Rembrandt's relations with the Reformed Church were undisturbed. Only after the birth of Cornelia did the situation become difficult. An important document in the minutes of the Amsterdam (Reformed) church council of 1654 states that Hendrickje Stoffels was living with Rembrandt illicitly. First Hendrickje and Rembrandt were summoned before the council. A week later it was stated that Hendrickje had not appeared. Rembrandt was no longer mentioned. After another two weeks it was decided that some brethren should go and see Hendrickje. At last she appeared before the council which reprimanded her severely, called her to penitence and determined that, for the time being, she should be 'banned from' communion.[26] We know the facts which made the council intervene. At the end of the forties Hendrickje had taken up service with Rembrandt. The legal and financial situation brought about by Saskia's will and by the high expenditure for the house and his collections did not permit Rembrandt to re-marry. As long as there were no children, all was well. But when Hendrickje gave birth to a girl (Cornelia), the Church intervened.

Why did the council first summon Hendrickje and Rembrandt together but deal with Hendrickje alone after that? It has been suggested that they realized that Rembrandt did not belong to the National Reformed Church. But a simpler explanation can be given. According to the documents, Cornelia was probably

born in 1651 or 1652.[27] The first consideration of the
council when it intervened must have been to get
the child baptized. The church discipline which was
then in force demanded that a child should be baptized
as soon as possible.

But that is a conclusion which is in conflict with a
number of other facts, such as Rembrandt's participa-
tion as witness in the baptism of his granddaughter
Titia in 1669 and his close relations with active members and even officials of the Reformed Church. Can
the attitude of the church council not be explained in
another way? In such disciplinary cases there are, at
least in theory, two main motives. One is to get the
man and woman living together without being married to see the error of their ways; the other is to ensure
that the child is baptized as soon as possible. Now the
second is really the most important. The Church
council had probably hoped that by exhorting the
parents they could get the situation remedied, but
they must have discovered that Rembrandt was in an
impossible situation or that he was not likely to
accept any exhortation. It seems that they now followed the line of least resistance. The child which is
expected must be baptized soon after its birth, but a
child born out of wedlock must not be baptized before
the mother has appeared before the council and been
invited to repent.[28] The result was that Cornelia was
baptized three months after Hendrickje's appearance
before the council.[29]

At any rate Rembrandt cannot have been a Mennonite in those years, for on account of his domestic
circumstances he could in no way be looked upon as a
member of a 'pure community'. Church discipline was

far severer among the Mennonites than in the Reformed Church, and could naturally be exercised more easily in their rather small congregations. A man who lived with a woman in an illicit relationship, had his child baptized in the Reformed Church and was a declared bankrupt would soon have been expelled again.[30]

Moreover, the Mennonites with whom he came into contact at this period of his life did not belong to the faithful representatives of the practice of their community. Van Hoogstraten, who had been Rembrandt's pupil, Coppenol whose portrait he etched twice and Catherina Hooghsaet whom he painted, were all in conflict with the discipline which the Mennonites sought to maintain so consistently. In fact at this time Rembrandt seems to have had little or no connection with any church. It is a striking fact that from the time of the summons from the church council there are no portraits of Reformed or Mennonite preachers, but only of Rabbis. It is tragic that at the very time when Rembrandt thrusts forward to the heart of the gospel he lived his life only on the fringe of the Church.

This does not, however, mean that he broke with the Church completely. If that were the case we would be unable to explain that—as we shall see in the next chapter—staunch churchmen like the Precentor Waterloos or Rector Heyblocq were among his friends, and that the orthodox minister Leupenius sent his young son to Rembrandt's studio. That he still looked upon himself as a member of the Reformed Church is confirmed by the fact that he was present as godfather at the baptism of his granddaughter in 1669. For the witnesses had, according to church discipline, to be men or women who professed 'the pure teaching'.

We must conclude from all this that Rembrandt's Christianity cannot be defined in terms of the Church, but is the result of his personal encounter with the Bible. He is not interested in systems and orthodoxies. The great stream of disputation about theological and philosophical problems passed him by.[31] He certainly learned from many people belonging to different confessions, but he remained independent. In his youth and at the time of his marriage with Saskia, the influence of the Reformed Church was predominant. In his forties he probably became more closely acquainted with Mennonite teachings. In his later years, as we shall see, he only kept up relations with a small circle of friends whose attitude, while framed by the Reformed creed, was that of a broad-minded and very personal biblical Christianity.

We cannot say, however, that any external influence was decisive for him. Nor is it to be expected. The painter who studied the models of classical and medieval art, of the Renaissance and Baroque art, and who at last created a style of his own, was not the man to be caught by some theological system or other. The only authority he recognized was the Bible. In that sense he was a Protestant, but a Protestant like the men of the sixteenth century who rediscovered the Bible and with joyous surprise found a new and fresh message in it; and not a Protestant in the sense of the churches of the seventeenth century which started systematizing the biblical message all over again.

CHAPTER EIGHT

Rembrandt's Friends in the Last Period of His Life

★ ★ ★

D ID Rembrandt live an isolated life in the last period of his life; had he no inner contact, at that time, with people whose religious attitude might have been near his own? We must look into this more closely.

His life in the fifties and sixties has sometimes been described as that of an almost complete recluse. Rudolf Eisler compares the old Rembrandt with the 'Lonely Man in Autumn'[1] in Mahler's *Song of the Earth*. It is true that at the time when the church council summoned Hendrickje Stoffels, and when his financial collapse took place, a number of former friends disappeared out of Rembrandt's life, and that Rembrandt's always slender associations with the 'official' cultural leaders of Amsterdam, were broken off almost entirely. Schmidt Degener has described this isolation in his *Rembrandt und der holländische Barock* in a dramatic way. But that does not mean that all his former friends turned away from him. Even in those years a number of men remained loyal to him. Houbraken tells us[2] that 'in the autumn of his life', Rembrandt associated mostly 'with common people' (*gemeene luiden*) and with artists. But that must be understood with a grain of salt. The friends of his last period did in fact not belong to the influential circles of the town, there was not a

single patrician or regent among them, no very successful artist, nor any of the scholars with latinized
names. His friends may have belonged to a petty bour-
geois circle, but on the other hand they were men who
had a lively interest in the intellectual and artistic life
of their time, and took part in it in their own way,
however modest.

The many biographers of Rembrandt have not
sufficiently taken into consideration the fact that
several of those friends and acquaintances of the
'autumn' of his life were not only connected with one
another as friends of Rembrandt, but also by common
interests and convictions. Let us try to describe those
associations.

First we have to ask what kind of men kept up
personal and friendly relations with Rembrandt from
about 1650, and, if they knew Rembrandt already, did
not break with him in the critical years from 1654 to
1656? We are not concerned with those whom
Rembrandt met only for professional reasons. We find
the following names: Abraham Francen, Christiaen
Dusart, Jeremias de Decker, H. F. Waterloos, Jacobus
Heyblocq, Gerbrandt van den Eeckhout, Aert de
Gelder, Heiman Dullaert, Roelant Roghman, the
Lutmas (father and son).[3]

In this list, we have to distinguish between those
whose relation to Rembrandt was very close, and those
who belonged to a wider circle of friends.

The first group, i.e. the group of intimate friends of
his family, includes Abraham Francen and Christiaen
Dusart. We know that those two men played a decisive
part in the life of Rembrandt and his family in his last
years. They were always ready to help him in any

financial or legal difficulties and at the end they became the trustees of Rembrandt's daughter Cornelia.

Abraham Francen was a pharmacist and an art dealer. We hear that he was a *'grand amateur d'Estampe'* and sometimes ate and drank little in order to save money for etchings which he wanted to acquire.[4] And indeed we see him, in Rembrandt's etching, with an engraving in his hand, and a triptych of the crucifixion is hanging on one wall of the room.[5] The documents prove that he was a faithful and reliable friend who assisted the artist often and readily by word and deed. His marriage had been solemnized in the Reformed Church in Amsterdam.[6] In 1670, in his capacity as Cornelia's guardian, he arranged the banns for her church wedding with Cornelis Suythof.[7] He therefore belonged to the Reformed Church.

When Christiaen Dusart was two years old, his family moved from Antwerp to Utrecht (1620) where his father became a town trumpeter. The father's offer to accompany the services with the cornet was accepted, and so he played in the Cathedral on holidays, and perhaps even more regularly. His children were baptized in the Reformed Church.[8] Joan Dusart, a brother of Christiaen's, was an organist in the 'Great Church' in Haarlem, and on his suggestion it was decided that the organ should be played regularly during the church services, as an accompaniment to the psalm-singing. Joan's son Cornelis became a well-known painter.[9]

Christiaen Dusart was a dyer in Amsterdam and seems to have done much travelling. He painted a number of portraits.[10] We learn from the documents that he was a friend of Rembrandt's family, certainly

73

from 1661, and that he stood by Rembrandt's side in an unselfish way. So he, too, became a guardian of Cornelia. And when Rembrandt died, it was he, along with Titus' widow, who 'out of the fear of God' lent the money which was needed to give Rembrandt a decent funeral.[11]

*   *   *

We now come to the second group.

Jeremias de Decker (1609-66) had grown up in poor circumstances and had, as he says himself, 'never heard the dollars jingle in his purse'. He was entirely self-taught, and had acquired a very considerable knowledge of languages, classics and theology, so that he was able to read and translate Latin, French, Italian and English authors. As a poet, he had a good reputation among his contemporaries, as we learn from remarks of Huygens, Vondel, Oudaen and Westerbaen. At a time when bombastic rhetoric and orgies of language were the fashion, he tried to speak a simple and clear language. He wrote to Westerbaen, 'There are people in this country who prefer roaring to speaking',[12] and he was probably thinking of Jan Vos and his imitators.

His best poems are those where he is speaking of his faith, like the one about the star of the Magi.[13] There we find stanzas which can compare with the best of his contemporaries. His best longer work is *The Passion of Jesus Christ* (*Good Friday*). This description of the Passion is especially impressive, because here the visual image and the message, representation and interpretation are most naturally joined together. Before our eyes he depicts the events of Good Friday, but he always takes part in it himself and knows 'il s'agit de nous et de notre tout' (Pascal). Christ suffers for us and in our place.

> *Uw' schuldeloose borge*
> *Heeft uwe schuld betaald*
>
> Your innocent bailsman
> Has paid your debt

But to imitate Christ means to carry one's own cross:

> *Men kan de vrucht van't Kruys*
> *Niet ongekruyst ontfaën.*
>
> Men cannot receive uncrucified
> The fruit of the cross.

Several contemporary poets commented on the special significance which that cycle had in the work of the poet and in the whole of Dutch Christian poetry.[14]

De Decker declared openly that he was concerned neither with formal beauty nor with the art of entertainment: 'I prefer you to learn rather than to laugh.'[15] The poet should use his gifts in the service:

> *Aen 't hervormen van de seden*
> *Of aen keur van bijbelstof*
>
> Of the reformation of manners
> Or of significant biblical themes.[16]

So it is not surprising that he is sometimes too ponderous for our liking.[17] But he is a sharp observer and describes the qualities and defects of his time with fine irony. In his *Praise of Avarice* he takes as a model Erasmus' *Praise of Folly* and ridicules the avarice of his contemporaries. The poem strikes us as surprisingly close to life when we think of Rembrandt's fate, for

75

very probably the poet was thinking of Rembrandt
when he wrote the following lines:

Als luck of geld verloopt, al houdt de deugde stand,
Soo stort de Vriendschap stracks op haren neus in 't sand.
Ich wist hierover heel wat staelkens op te halen.

As luck or money runs out, though virtue may still stand,
So friendship straightway falls with her nose in the sand.
I could tell many a tale about that.[18]

De Decker belonged to the Reformed Church.
He admits, regretfully, that he does not go to church
as often as he should. But he seems to have worshipped
frequently in the French Reformed Church. When the
French minister Hotton died, de Decker wrote a
poem in which he spoke very gratefully of his sermons,
which he had often heard. He did not want to have
anything to do with scholastic exaggeration of the
doctrine of predestination, but he thought the ministers should indulge less in polemics, and more in
edification. He praises the orthodox minister Langhelius, however, who 'fought with the help of God's
word, as with an iron sword, against atheism'.[19] To
the Arminian Westerbaen who had thought de Decker
would embrace the Arminian faith, he wrote that he did
not see any reason for leaving the Reformed Church.[20]
The defence of Protestantism was his great concern.[21]

We do not know exactly when the friendship between Rembrandt and de Decker began, but it is
likely that this was in or before 1638. For de Decker
visited Rembrandt at the time when he was painting
the *Christ appearing to Mary Magdalen* for Waterloos.

Rembrandt painted him more than once. There
must have been a portrait painted before 1660. For in

that year Waterloos published a poem dedicated to Rembrandt 'at the time when he painted the profound poet de Decker'.[22]

The portrait of 1666 (in the Hermitage, Leningrad) is well known, for it is one of the last which Rembrandt painted, and demonstrates his power of penetration into the very life of another person at its height. A contemporary, J. van Petersom, saw this when he wrote:

O Rembrandt, schoon Uw vlijt de Decker heeft gemaelt
Zoo konstig dat de ziel als uit het aenschijn straelt, ...

O Rembrandt, by your zeal you paint de Decker so
That his soul shines through his face ...

In his poem of thanks[23] for Rembrandt's second portrait of him de Decker stresses that Rembrandt has painted it only out of friendship and love of the Muses, not in order to earn money with it. He assures us that if he had the power he would describe Rembrandt's work in verse and, in defiance of envy,[24] depict before men's eyes Rembrandt's noble spirit. He emphasizes that Rembrandt's fame has flown over the Alps to Rome and that he has surpassed Raphael and Michelangelo. These words have a special significance, as de Decker did not speak like that about any other painter. We must give him great credit for understanding the importance of Rembrandt's art at a time when almost all other poets honoured Rubens as the summit of art and advocated a pseudo-classical aesthetics of external forms. De Decker's poem about the painting, *Christ appearing to Mary Magdalen* will be discussed later.

H. F. Waterloos was a precentor and visitor in the service of the Reformed Church. Usually this post was very badly paid and held by uneducated men. Waterloos

must have been an exception, for he had made himself sufficiently at home in the world of literature
to occupy a not inconsiderable place among the poets
of his time. His friend Cornelia van der Veer described
him as 'Cantor in the House of God and shaker of
consciences' who

> *een ziel hoe baugh te moe kon streelen*
> *Met sulcken sachten hand, dat zelfs het wreetst gemoet*
> *Versmolt in tranen tot berouw en ware boet.*

> *Can soothe the soul however full of fear*
> *With such a soft touch that the hardest heart*
> *Must melt in tears of true contrition.*

and, at the same time, as the 'high-minded poet'

> *Waar d' IJ-stadt meer op roemt als Rotterdam op't Beeldt*
> *Van Desideer . . .*

> *Whose fame exceeds that of the sage of Rotterdam,*
> *Of Desiderius* (i.e. Desiderius Erasmus).

His poems appeared in a number of collections. These
deal largely with biblical themes. At the same time he
sang the praises of the Amsterdam ministers.[25] In the
'Hollandsche Parnas' we find his poems on everyone
of the 'orthodox' pastors of the Reformed Church of
Amsterdam.

He is too fond of the 'language of Canaan' and the
'language of Parnassus', so that his poems often lack
simplicity and straightforwardness. But he is not
simply a producer of rhyme. It is possible to discover in
his poetry the heart and mind of a deeply religious man
who lives by and for his Bible-centred convictions.

At all events he must have had a good name among
the poets of his time. Even Huygens printed some of
his poems. He wrote at least three poems about works

of Rembrandt's: about the first portrait of Jeremias de Decker, about the small Coppenol etching, and about the *Hundred Guilder Print*. We know that Rembrandt painted a *Mary Magdalen* for him because de Decker tells us in his poem.[26] Waterloos was also in Rembrandt's studio when he began to paint de Decker, and in his schoolmasterly way he advises Rembrandt to consider well that he sees before him not an unimportant man but a great poet. If Rembrandt should succeed in immortalizing the poet, Waterloos' poetic art would remain alive in Rembrandt's paintings, and vice versa, Rembrandt's 'art of drawing' in Waterloos' song.[27]

It was characteristic of the attitude of the poets of that time, as well as of Waterloos' personal attitude, that he exhorted Rembrandt in such a fatherly way. A comparison of this poem with the one he made about a portrait of the minister Langhelius by Frans Hals, shows his real esteem of Rembrandt. For there we read:

> *Wat pooght gij, oude Hals, Langhelius te maalen*
> *Uw ooghen zijn te zwak voor zijn gheleerde straalen*[28]
>
> *Why do you try, old Hals, to paint Langhelius?*
> *Your eyes are too weak for the rays of his genius*

It is important that Waterloos was a friend of Rembrandt's before the disciplinary investigation of the Church and his financial breakdown, as well as afterwards. Rembrandt painted for him a *Mary Magdalen* in the thirties, but Waterloos published in 1660 his poems about the portrait of de Decker and the Coppenol etching. Hence he did not disown his relationship with Rembrandt. That this servant of the Church proclaimed his high esteem for Rembrandt before all the world at that time, is not without significance.

The father of Jacobus Heyblocq (1623-73 or later) was the caretaker of a school in Amsterdam; but his son was allowed to study theology with the help of the municipal government in Leyden. When he finished his studies, there was no vacancy in the Reformed Church, so he became a preceptor, and later rector of the grammar-school. But he did not give up preaching, and also his poetry shows that he remained faithful to theology. Even his grief about the death of his friend (the minister of Gorkum) was dressed in theological thought forms:

> *Nu leeft Gij, daar Gij niet kunt dwaalen*
> *En in U houwt het erf quaat op.*[29]

> *Now you live where you cannot err*
> *And original sin in you has ceased.*

He wrote Dutch and Latin poems, e.g. on the first petition of the Lord's Prayer, and the persecution of the Waldensians in Piedmont, though, in fact, he had but slender poetic gifts. His real artistic achievement consisted in the assembling in his house of men from very different walks of life. That is why his *Album Amicorum* is unique.

In this Album, Rembrandt drew a magnificent representation of *Simeon with the Christ Child* in the year 1661.[30] The eyes of this Simeon have truly seen the Saviour, and he can say '*Nunc dimittis*'. Beside the picture there is a poem signed 'A.L.', to which we shall return later.

The fact that this drawing has been given especial prominence by the accompanying poem[31] indicates Heyblocq's admiration for Rembrandt's art. This is proved by an undated poem where Heyblocq calls the 'great' Coppenol etching Rembrandt's masterpiece.[32]

As this album also contains very friendly poems by a number of men who were closely connected with Rembrandt, we must assume that Heyblocq can be numbered among Rembrandt's friends at that time. It is possible though that their acquaintance began in 1658, for the first indication of their association is Heyblocq's poem on the Coppenol etching of (about) 1658.

Gerbrand van den Eeckhout (1621-74) had been Rembrandt's pupil between about 1635 and 1640. His family belonged to the Dutch Reformed Church, and he had been baptized in that Church. Houbraken counts him among the master's best pupils who painted in Rembrandt's style for the whole of his life.[33] This is not quite correct as in later years van den Eeckhout sometimes followed the new academic style, especially in his portraits. But his numerous biblical works show how decisive Rembrandt's spiritual influence was for him to the end of his life. The biblical themes chosen by him are practically all Rembrandt's themes. It is easy to see how much he is dominated by the memory of Rembrandt. Compare, for instance, his painting *The Raising of Jairus' Daughter* (Berlin) with Rembrandt's drawing (also at Berlin).[34] Quite obviously the figure of Christ as seen by Rembrandt had caught his imagination. He may be called an epigone,[35] and it is certain too that he sometimes allowed himself to be tempted to follow the academic fashion. But all the same he did try, to the best of his admittedly limited abilities, to carry on in the spirit of his master. Therefore it does not surprise us that up to a few years ago the series of drawings in which he represented the whole story of Joseph were assured to be Rembrandt's.[36]

Houbraken also tells us that after his apprenticeship, van den Eeckhout remained Rembrandt's friend. It is tragic that we can report this of three pupils only: Eeckhout, de Gelder and Dullaert. But at any rate these three have shown in their works (Dullaert more in poetry than in painting) that they had not only learnt the secrets of the technique of painting from Rembrandt, but something more, a message about God and man.[37]

Though Aert de Gelder (1645-1727) stayed only two years with Rembrandt (around 1661, according to Lilienfeld), and though be belonged to a much younger generation, he must be mentioned here, because more than any other he remained a faithful pupil, and carried on the tradition of Rembrandt's biblical art into the eighteenth century.[38] As late as forty years after his apprenticeship, he painted a self-portrait, in which he is seen holding the *Hundred Guilder Print*.[39] Of his three hundred known paintings, more than one hundred are biblical representations (half of which treat themes of the Old Testament). Houbraken and Weyerman tell us that he was a pious man and went regularly to (the Reformed) Church.

May we also count Heiman Dullaert (1636-84) among Rembrandt's friends at that time? Houbraken tells us that after only a few years of apprenticeship in Rembrandt's studio, he later kept in touch with the master and his pupils. The question is, what does this 'later' mean? We know that Dullaert lived in Rembrandt's house in 1653. It is likely that he stayed in Amsterdam as late as 1658[40] and soon after returned to Rotterdam, his native city. Does Houbraken mean that, during his stay in Amsterdam, even after the time he spent in Rembrandt's studio, he remained associated with him? Or that in his later years in Rotterdam too, he cultivated his friendship with his master? We do not know for certain. Perhaps Weyerman is right in saying that he only kept up a correspondence with his old friends. It is hardly likely that the ailing Dullaert should have left Rotterdam again once he had returned there. But even though he may only have spent five years in Rembrandt's company, he shall be named here, for his art, especially his poetry, is closely related to Rembrandt's art.

Dullaert was really more of a poet than a painter. Only few of his paintings have survived, and these are not of great importance. As a poet, though, he ranks with the very foremost. A modern poet has said of him that his poems display a beauty so deeply experienced in their personal concrete presentation of biblical events that they are worthy of the chiaroscuro of Rembrandt.[41] And indeed we cannot read his work without being reminded of Rembrandt. Who does not think of the cosmic struggle between light and darkness as it is represented in the etching *Three Crosses*, when reading:

En ik ga door de dood uit mijne duisternissen
Naar 't onuitbluschlijk licht, dat in den Hemel schijnt.

And I go through death, out of my darkness,
To the unextinguishable light shining in heaven.

In Dullaert's work religious poetry takes the first place. These poems which are expressions of his faith are not discursive treatises, but dramatic representations of the Bible story. This is especially true of the great poem about St Peter, which describes the whole drama of Peter's life with deep sensitivity. Wille has

83

shown us that there is probably a relation between this poem and Rembrandt's etching of 1645.[42] Rembrandt represents Peter gazing at the key entrusted to him by Jesus with bitter, ironical self-accusation. The same theme is to be found in Dullaert's poem:

Dat Petrus, door de macht van U on opgeleit
Aan andren nog het Hof des Hemels open stelle,
Hij die zelf klopt en schelt aan't nachtportaal der helle,
Hij, die U heeft verzaakt, dat is het al gezeit.[43]

That Peter, through the power given by you,
Is to open the garden of heaven to others,
He who himself knocks and rings at the dark gate of Hell,
He who has forsaken you, this has been made known to
the world.

Dullaert also took an active part in the life of the Church. He belonged to the French Reformed congregation in Rotterdam and was a deacon from 1666 to 1667, and an elder from 1671 to 1678. But we learn from his poems about Simonides and Lemaire that he was on friendly terms with ministers of the Dutch Reformed Church in Rotterdam too. We can also get to know Dullaert's convictions from the translations he made. As an elder of the French congregation he naturally had a special interest in Huguenot literature, so he translated two French books which played a great part in the religious life of the time.[44]

In 1663 Charles Drélincourt, the well-known Reformed minister in Charenton, had written his reply to the letter of the Landgrave Ernest of Hesse to the ministers of Charenton. Landgrave Ernest had become a Roman Catholic in 1652. Drélincourt had known him before his conversion and was deeply shocked at his abandonment of the Protestant faith. His book is an earnest admonition joined with polemic of a very high order. The real point is whether the Bible is to have the first and last word or not. In the discussion of these things it no longer matters to him that he is speaking to a prince: 'You were armed with the sword of the Spirit, which is the Word of the living God; but you have wretchedly forsaken Him on the day of battle. Your Highness has given himself over to error, superstition and false service as cowardly—forgive me this word—as if you had never beheld this divine book, or as if in a moment, you had forgotten all its mysteries, and all its instructions. In the whole of your letter, which comprises twenty-three large pages, I have not found a single word of the Scriptures. . . .'[45] Drélincourt emphasizes that the Reformed Church has nothing to do with the sects, for 'we believe that it is folly to boast of possessions of a peculiar spirit'.[46]

The second book translated by Dullaert is Pierre Du Moulin's *Traité de la Paix de l'Ame et du Contentement de l'Esprit*.[47] Du Moulin was the son of a Reformed theologian who in 1615 had tried to interest James I of England in his work for church unity, but at the time of the Synod of Dordrecht had sharply attacked the Remonstrants. His son had had to flee from France to England. His book which was widely read, and even praised by Pierre Bayle,[48] reflects an Anglican and Humanist way of thinking, He is concerned with a peaceful synthesis of theology and philosophy, of faith and ethics, and seeks to abolish the sharp contrasts which had dominated the thought of the first post-reformation generation. He addresses himself to men who are weary of religious battles and seek inner peace. He will have nothing to do with scholasticism.[49] In religious things, one should stick to what is clearly revealed to us, and leave aside everything uncertain and difficult. One should live in peace with all those who accept the fundamental articles.[50] His thought does not soar high, and does not dig deep. He teaches a sober wisdom which is rooted in the Bible, but at the same time derives from other classical sources. It must be this union of Christian revelation and classical wisdom which specially attracted Dullaert in this book.

Of Roelant Roghman (1597-1686 or 1687) we do not know very much. He must have led a very independent life. We do not find him in official society nor in the companies of the painters. He almost completely restricted himself to objective representations of scenery, towns and villages, and did more drawing than painting. Here, however, he is so close to Rembrandt that some critics say that he influenced Rembrandt, others, that Rembrandt influenced him. And indeed some of his paintings have long been taken for genuine Rembrandts. He died in complete destitution. The only work of his handed down to us shows that he did not make things easy for himself. He states:

Als men de dingen komt te weten, is men versleten.

When man comes to know about things, he is worn out.

Houbraken tells us that when one of Roghman's pupils in the last years of Rembrandt's life wished to become his pupil, Rembrandt refused him, saying that he and Roghman were such good friends that he did not want to take away his pupils.

The Lutmas were goldsmiths. Lutma the Elder designed the choir-screen for the *Nieuwe Kerk* in

Amsterdam. The etching Rembrandt made of him in 1656 tells us more about him than the few surviving documents.[51] At that time Lutma must have been a kind and wise old man. As copperplate-engravers he and his son (1624-85) were in a sense colleagues of Rembrandt, and the three were probably fond of each other's company. Lutma was also interested in biblical art. On a wedding medallion[52] he represented 'Eliezer and Rebekah at the Well', a theme treated several times by Rembrandt in his drawings. Rembrandt also painted his son.[53]

This Joannes Lutma the Younger was a painter himself. According to Bredius it is not impossible that he was a pupil of Rembrandt. His inventory names two portraits by Rembrandt, probably self-portraits.[54]

The Lutmas belonged to the Reformed Church. The marriage of the father with Sara de Bie was registered in the church on 18th May 1638.[55]

We must add a word about Lieven Willemsz van Coppenol. The older literature on Rembrandt sometimes numbered him among Rembrandt's friends; but Mr H. F. Wijnman's careful examination of his life shows that this is impossible.[56] We now know that this schoolmaster and calligrapher was so incredibly ambitious that he may only be excused on the assumption that he was a psychopath. We assume that practically all the great and small poets of his time sang his praises, not only because he was indeed a master of calligraphy, but also because they pitied him, or were possibly paid for their rhymes. With Wijnman we must suppose that the two etchings as well as the painting in which Rembrandt immortalized him, date from the year 1658, and that Rembrandt probably painted him more than once because Coppenol was not pleased with the first execution of his commission.

Thus we cannot number him among Rembrandt's friends for certain, and the wonderful (large) Coppenol etching must rather be looked upon as a striking example of Rembrandt's ability, in his painting to endow a man, as it were, with a new existence.

The fact that Coppenol was a Mennonite is of no importance, or only of negative importance, when we examine Rembrandt's relations with the Mennonites. When in 1656 Coppenol was summoned twice by the deacons of the Mennonite congregation to answer for his debauched life, he did not appear,[57] and the deacons sighed, 'God grant that he may improve.'[58]

Several of Rembrandt's friends like de Decker, Waterloos and Heyblocq, composed panegyrics to Coppenol. But when we hear that he had his portrait printed, framed by no less than twenty-eight eulogies,[59] we find it difficult to take a single one of them seriously.

Now most of these men were connected not only with Rembrandt, but also with one another. Not all of them, however: de Gelder belongs to a much younger generation, Dusart seems to have travelled widely, and we know little about the relations between Francen and Roghman. But we do know especially of de Decker, Waterloos, Heyblocq, van den Eeckhout and Dullaert (as long as he stayed in Amsterdam), that they were connected by a network of relationships.

In 1658 there appeared in Amsterdam an anthology *Het Gebedt onzes Heeren* in which nine poets published detailed poems on the different petitions of the Lord's Prayer. 'A heavenly sanctuary is opened' here, as the printer says, under the patronage of three Reformed ministers. Of Rembrandt's friends, de Decker, Waterloos and Dullaert contributed.[60] The nine poets seem to have formed a work-group of Reformed poets in order to bring out their anthology.[61]

This anthology was dedicated, on behalf of all the collaborators, to the 'learned' and 'thoughtful' professor of mathematics, Alexander de Bie. We find the name of this professor in the *Album* of Jacobus Heyblocq, in 1664, and in 1689 as the executor of the will of Joannes Lutma Junior.

The statesman and poet Constantijn Huygens, who in his youth had 'discovered' Rembrandt, was admired by de Decker, and accepted the co-operation of Waterloos. He visited Heyblocq at the time when Rembrandt made the drawing of Simeon in his *Album*.[62] It is not impossible that Huygens and Rembrandt thus saw each other again after a long time.

De Decker and Heyblocq were friends of the poet Westerbaen. De Decker wrote an eulogy on the book of the French minister Marmet, whose sermons were translated by Dullaert.

According to Houbraken, Eeckhout was on specially friendly terms with Roghman whose portrait he painted.

Lutma and Eeckhout collaborated to edit a collection of ornamental engravings which, as Neumann has shown, are very close to Rembrandt's work.[63]

Heyblocq's *Album Amicorum* confirms the fact that several of Rembrandt's friends were connected with one another. Admittedly their names are to be found among a great number of names of theologians, poets and painters, and certain pages of the *Album* are rather a collection of autographs than testimonies of true friendship. All the same, some of Rembrandt's friends figure here in a special way, in expressions that bear a very personal character. Eeckhout not only supplies a drawing, but also two poems. Waterloos praises Heyblocq for bringing up the young generation in the Christian faith. There is de Decker with a *Puntdicht* written in Coppenol's calligraphy,[64] and a poem on Heyblocq. He says quite soberly that Heyblocq serves art by laying the foundation of language in his teaching. And in Heyblocq's anthology *Farrago Latino-Belgica* the names of Waterloos and de Decker appear again.[65]

Waterloos sings the praises of de Decker,[66] and de Decker of Waterloos.[67] These men are in danger of admiring one another too much, as tends to happen in a circle of like-minded men of letters.

It is significant that the contemporary opinions which show a real understanding of Rembrandt's importance as an expounder of the Bible, come from this very circle. We have three of such testimonies.[68]

First, in a copy of *The Hundred Guilder Print* in Paris there are four short poems by H. F. Waterloos in which he tries to express what Rembrandt represents. He sees here, in brief, a proclamation of the biblical message. According to him, Rembrandt means to show the miracles God's Son has performed: the crucified and risen Messiah is the central theme. In the second poem he describes exactly which biblical texts were used by Rembrandt for this etching. As he was a friend of Rembrandt, it is quite possible that he just reports what Rembrandt told him. He says:

Hier hellept Jezus handt den zieken. En de kindren

*(Dat's Godtheyt!) zaalicht hij: En strafft ze die'r
    verhind'ren*
*Maar (ach!) den Jong'ling treurt. De schriftgeleerden
    smaalen*
't Geloof der heiligen, en Christi godtheits straalen.[69]

*Here Jesus' hand is helping the sick. And he is blessing
The children (that's divinity!): and punishing those that
    want to interfere,*
*But alas! the youth is grieving. The scribes are belittling
The faith of the saints, and the rays of Christ's divinity.*

For Waterloos, then, the *Hundred Guilder Print* is an
exposition of the nineteenth chapter of St Matthew, in
which Rembrandt reproduces the whole substance of
the chapter and renders witness to Christ as the Saviour
of men.

The second important testimony is a poem by Jeremias
de Decker on a painting called *Christ and Mary Magdalen*
which Rembrandt had painted for Waterloos. De
Decker visited Rembrandt while he was working at it.[70]

It is most likely that this poem refers to the painting
of 1638. For the only other painting dealing with this
passage of St John is clearly a representation of the
moment when Jesus says to Mary: 'Noli me tangere.'
And de Decker refers to an earlier part of the passage.[71]

What then does de Decker say? He emphasizes that
Rembrandt more than any other painter brings the
scriptures to life. He interprets Rembrandt's intention
in these words:

't schijnt dat de Christus segt: Marie en wilt niet beven,
Ick ben't de dood en heeft aan uwen Heer geen deel:
Sij sulx geloovende, maar echter nocht niet heel,
*Schijnt tusschen vreugde en druck; en vreese en hoop te
    sweven.*[72]

Christ seems to say 'Mary, thou shalt not fear,
It is I. Death has no part in your Lord':
She believes it, but not yet wholly,
And seems to be suspended between joy and care, between
   fear and hope.

Thus the poet who in the next lines addresses Rembrandt as a friend testifies that Rembrandt has not conceived the story of Mary Magdalene as an interesting theme with aesthetic possibilities; but that he tries to represent what St John's Gospel really has to say here. So for de Decker Rembrandt is a reliable expositor of the Scriptures.

The third testimony is to be found in Jacobus Heyblocq's *Album Amicorum*. A certain A.L. has written a poem on the wonderful drawing *Simeon with the Christ Child*,[73] and the first lines run as follows:

Hier toont ons Rembrandt hoe den ouden Simeon
Met vreucht, syn Heylant en Messias neemt in d'armen
En nu omt' sterven wenst, wijl sijn genaden son
   Verschenen is.[74]

Here Rembrandt shows us how old Simeon
With joy takes his Saviour and Messiah into his arms
And now wants to die, because the sun of his mercy
   Has shone forth.

He adds that this may teach us that pious people need not fear death. So this poet, too, is convinced that in his pictures Rembrandt interprets the biblical word in its actual meaning.

Who wrote this poem? In 1877 Vosmaer suggested that A.L. might be the initials of A. Lydius, without giving any reasons. Probably he had in mind that Heyblocq was closely associated with the Lydius family, that several members of this family, who (according to Pierre Bayle) had furnished the Church with more ministers than any other, had inscribed themselves in his *Album*, and that Jacobus Lydius[75] had been with Heyblocq on 18th March 1661, i.e. two weeks before A.L. wrote his poem in the album. But it is impossible to prove the existence of an A. Lydius who might have written such a poem.[76]

A.L. may mean 'Amicus Lydius' or 'Amicus Leidensis', and so it may stand for a Lydius after all. But there is another possibility.

In those years there lived in Amsterdam a certain A. B. de Leeuw, an actor who was also a poet and who mostly called himself A. Leeuw. He translated several plays, mostly from the French and was a friend of the poet and innkeeper Jan Soet. In this circle he had quite a reputation as a poet. In one of the poetical contests which Jan Soet organized Leeuw received the first prize for his answer to the question: 'What is commonest in the world and least appreciated?' The main theme of his answer was:

> *De Zegen Gods is met geen tal te noemen.*
> *Zij is in alle ding.*
>
> God's blessings are uncountable
> They are in everything.

In another collection of poems, *The Contest between Catharina Questiers and Cornelia* (1665), we find again a poem signed 'A.L'. It is most probable that these are again the initials of Leeuw, for several of his friends from the circle of Jan Soet contributed to this collection. Now in the years 1661 and 1662 Jan Soet three times wrote poems in the Heyblocq *Album* and he may well have brought his friend Leeuw along too. This is all the more likely as in the years 1661-4 a number of poets who worked for the Amsterdam stage wrote their names in the Heyblocq *Album*: Asselijn, Focquenbrock, J. Dullaert, Blasius.

This does not imply that the poet who wrote these lines necessarily shared the strange views of Jan Soet; many different opinions were held in his house. The true head of the group was H. Bruno,[77] a theologian who had been tutor in the family of Constantijn Huygens; another member was Steendam. The group did not hold together very long because its members began to quarrel.

We have seen that there was a group of men around Rembrandt who were associated with him as well as with one another. Was there then a Rembrandt circle? Surely not in the technical sense. This was no artists' fraternity of the kind Martin Kretser founded in 1654 (which Rembrandt did not join). Nor was it a debating club like the one Jan Soet arranged in his inn, nor a 'college' after the model of the Collegiants. This circle of Rembrandt's friends was no more and no less than a group of men who liked to be in one another's company because they had the same artistic and religious interests and also because they may not have felt at home in the other numerous circles and groups which existed in their city. That is, it was in no way a closed circle, with the character of a club or association. They were just men who looked for an intellectual atmosphere akin to their own. What brought these men together? What was common to all of them?

First we can say that with the exception of Heyblocq, who had a university education, they were typically self-taught men. They did not belong to the world of scholars, but they had acquired an extensive knowledge and used their own free and individual judgment. None of them was the exponent of a party or fashion. We cannot easily classify them in the history of culture, especially in the religious field. As we have already seen they looked upon themselves as Reformed Christians and members of the National Church, but this does not mean that their attitude towards this Church was uncritical.

De Decker called the dogmatic strife about the doctrine of predestination 'a clumsy, even ungodly misunderstanding'[78] and recommended to the ministers:

Op dat ghy my beweegt, beweegt uselven eerst.[79]

In order to move me, move yourselves first.

He further proved his independence by protesting, long before Balthasar Bekker, against sorcery and witch-trials.[80] Dullaert translated du Moulin's *Traité de la Paix de l'Ame*, in which we find the complaint that since the Reformation nothing has been achieved for the conversion of the nations[81] by the strife among the Churches. Waterloos emphasizes that 'eternal Paradise' takes the first place, 'the external Church' only the second.[82] This attitude was conditioned by their desire to keep the windows open towards all sides. They did not dream of hiding behind the walls of creeds and theologies. According to de Decker 'God has his friends everywhere'.[83] Dullaert was a friend of the Collegiant Joachim Oudaen, who incidentally ushered in de Decker's anthology with an eulogy. Heyblocq was successful in maintaining his relation with people from very different quarters.

Professors, ministers, poets and painters came to his house and inscribed their names in his *Album Amicorum*.[84]

Only in the fifties and sixties do we first find the names of a number of professors and ministers who are champions of church orthodoxy: the aggressive polemicist Maresius, the enemies of Cartesian philosophy Martin Schoockius and Paulus Voet, Vondel's adversary Petrus Leupenius,[85] the enemy of the Jesuits, Jacobus Lydius, the ministers Laurentius and Caspar Streso.

Thus it seems that in the choice of his theological friends, Heyblocq's criterion was orthodoxy. But at the same time he welcomed poets and painters, and he was broadminded in matters of art. For there were representatives of very different currents among the poets he invited. The *Album* contains poems by well-known Reformed poets such as Huygens, de Decker, Anna Maria van Schurman, or the less famous like Waterloos and H. Bruno. But we also find contributions from the versatile innkeeper Jan Soet, who indulged in the most sarcastic remarks about all the churches and sects. It even happened that on 10th September 1660 the court preacher Caspar Streso, leading polemicist against the Arminians, came for a visit, and two days later Jacob Westerbaen, an Arminian, who in his poems sharply attacked the Reformed preachers. Comenius, Bishop of the Czech Moravian Church, pedagogue and protagonist of church unity, was also a guest of Heyblocq, in 1656.

As we have seen, de Decker had a special partiality for the sermons of Godefroy Hotton, a preacher of the French congregation in Amsterdam.[86] In his *Praise of*

Avarice he describes how Hotton sharply attacked the idolatry of money in a sermon.[87] But he must have respected Hotton so very highly because he was a champion of Church unity, and especially of an understanding between the Reformed Church and the Lutheran. For Hotton took a part in the ecumenical efforts of Comenius, de Geer and Duraeus. In his little book about true tolerance,[88] he summons the Churches to emphasize only what is necessary for salvation. But he refused to accept the Socinians and Baptists in the united evangelical Church. Because of his irenical attitude he was sharply attacked by Professor Spanheim.

As to Roman Catholicism, we find an open ear for the contributions of individual Roman Catholic views joined with a strict rejection of the Roman system. Thus Dullaert translated the Roman Catholic de la Serre and praised François van Hoogstraten's translation of *Worldly Vanities* by the Franciscan Didacus Stella.[89] But he also published the stout defence of Protestant faith by Charles Drélincourt and prayed for the conversion of papacy.[90] De Decker knew his Erasmus and profited by him, but he also wrote a long poem on the pact between the pope and the devil[91] and was deeply revolted by the persecution of the Waldensians.[92] Heyblocq invited the Roman Catholics Vondel and Anslo to write in his *Album*, but wrote a poem called *Crown of Martyrs*,[93] in which the suffering of the Waldensians, and their struggle for freedom of faith is described. Waterloos was in touch with the Roman Catholic Jan Vos.

The Christian attitude represented by these men shows neither the hard, dogmatic petrifaction of so many Reformed sermons of that time, nor the soft

sentimentality of the champions of the thorough-going
spiritualism which was then arising. Their attitude was
firmly grounded in the Bible, but was also strongly
personal. In Dullaert's poems it is striking how the line
of thought always begins with the story of salvation
and wins through in the end to personal decision. In
describing the dying of Christ, he first paints the cross
before our eyes:

Die alles troost en laaft, verzucht, bezwijmt, ontverft,
Die alles ondersteunt geraakt, o mij! aan't wijken.
Een doodsche donkerheid komt voor zijn oogen strijken
Die quijnen, als een roos die dauw en warmte derft.

He who comforts and refreshes all, sighs, goes out,
grows pale,
He who supports all, begins, alas, to stagger
A deadly darkness crowds before his eyes
Which languish like a rose that longs for dew and warmth.

What the Cross means for the poet personally, is
expressed in the third stanza:

Daar hij het leven derft, wil ik het ook gaan derven:
Maar hoe hij meerder sterft, en ik meer wil gaan sterven,
Hoe mij een voller stroom van leven overvloeit

As he gives up his life, I will give up mine too:
But the more he dies and the more I will die,
The more a full stream of life flows in me.

In de Decker's poems we also find this reciprocity,
so that a purely descriptive poem grows into a dia-
logue between God and man. He makes it very clear
how the scholastic intellectualism of orthodoxy destroys
true faith. In a short poem on *The Religion (Godsdien-*
stigheyd) of our Time[94] he writes in his ironical way:

De Liefde is nu in praet en niet in daed gelegen:
't Geloove hangt van 't vernuft, niet van Schriftuur, so 't
pleeg;
De Godsdienst is van t'hert na 't herssenhuys gestegen;
In 't herssen huyst hij nu, en 't hert helaes! staet leeg.

Love now consists in word and not in deed,
Faith depends on reason, not on the Scriptures, as it
used to be;
Religion has ascended from the heart to the head
It now dwells in the brains, and the heart, alas! is
empty.

In other words, these men were concerned with a biblical Christianity. Decker says one should not talk so light-heartedly of things about which the Scriptures speak so soberly.[95] They lived with their Bible and always had the stories of the Old and New Testaments before their eyes. These stories were their own stories. Thus Waterloos speaks of the grief he felt when he read de Decker's *Good Friday*. In the Bible they first and foremost realized 'the high wonder' of the incarnation and the cross. The unending paradox of this event was stressed again and again, in language which with some justice has been compared with the *chiaroscuro* of Rembrandt. The following lines by de Decker, as well as the above poem by Dullaert on the dying of Christ, may serve as an example:

Ach, ach, die 't all vertroost, staet hier van troost
versteken
Die 't all verlost, geboeyt; die 't all geneest, gewond.[96]
Alas, alas! He who comforts all, stands here without
any comfort
He who frees all, in chains, he who heals all, wounded.

They saw the whole world *sub specie aeternitatis*, and the transitoriness of human life was deeply impressed on their minds. That does not mean that they denied the place of culture. On the contrary, de Decker translated Horace and Ovid, and his *Praise of Avarice* contains innumerable quotations from the classical writers. Heyblocq wrote Latin poems, Dullaert translated du Bellay, Eeckhout drew the figures of Hercules and Hermes in the Heyblocq *Album*. Even the precentor Waterloos goes so far as to praise de Decker 'in the church of Apollo' and gives an interpretation in prose of a poem which is devoted to the activities of Cupid. But the whole circle agreed that culture and art are not ends in themselves. Their common aim, as Waterloos wrote in one of his poems on the *Hundred Guilder Print*, was:[97]

> *Op dat de Werelt zouw na zestien eeuwen zien,*
> *De wond'ren die hij aan haar allen heeft bedreven.*

> *That the world, after sixteen centuries, may see*
> *The wonders he has done unto all of them.*

Their attitude towards the world of culture is clearly formulated in Dullaert's work. Thus we read in du Moulin's *Traité*, which he translated, that 'all the beauty and all the variety of nature witness explicitly that God is an indulgent father who takes great pains to please and delight us'.[98] Therefore one should not pray, 'Lord, do me the favour not to please me in any worldly thing', but rather, that our eyes may be turned to

> *Daar starren, rijk aan glans, die als getuigen staan,*
> *De groote heerlijkheid van haren Schepper loven,*
> *En zeggen overluit: de schoonheyt is hier boven.*[99]

Where brilliant stars, standing there as witnesses,
Praise the great glory of their maker,
And loudly call: beauty is up here.

We may now draw some conclusions.

It must have meant a great deal to Rembrandt that he was not alone in these years. He had hardly any more contact with the 'official' world.[100] The circles which dominated the cultural life of Amsterdam only rarely took notice of him. So it must have been a comfort to him that a group of true friends remained to him. He must have appreciated the value of the friendship of men like de Decker, Waterloos and Heyblocq, who had a respected place in church circles. For the 'Dominie' Heyblocq and the precentor Waterloos it cannot have been a matter of course to associate with a man like Rembrandt who, in virtue of his domestic situation and his economic difficulties, was, socially speaking, an outsider.

Rembrandt must have realized clearly that these men had not gone far in the world. They belonged to the strata of the petty bourgeoisie and had little influence. He must have noticed their faults too: de Decker's inferiority complexes, Waterloos' exaggerated pompousness. But he must have found a community here which in the closing years of his life, was more important for him than any influential connections.

Of course we cannot assert that Rembrandt's Christianity was formed by his intercourse with these friends, for the constant intercourse with the Bible, and bitter experience, had before this led him on the way to the Gospels. But he must have rejoiced in the community he found here, especially in religious matters. We may assume that he received many an inspiration for his work in the conversations, and perhaps in the poems, of these friends.

Did these friends grasp the true significance of Rembrandt's art? We can only say that at least they grasped more of it than their contemporaries. They realized that Rembrandt was not just one of the many good contemporary painters. Jan Vos named Rembrandt among all sorts of known and unknown Amsterdam painters of his time.[101] But Jeremias de Decker dared to compare Rembrandt to Raphael and Michelangelo, and even though we take into account the rhetoric of the time, and his friendship for Rembrandt, he must have been convinced that Rembrandt surpassed all the artists of his time.

But it is more important that in this circle,—and we may add, in this circle only—the importance of Rembrandt as the painter of the Bible was realized. Not, of course, that they understood Rembrandt's art in all its depth. Who can say of himself that he has done as much as that? But at least it means that in Rembrandt they not only saw the great master of the technique of painting, but also that they became aware that he was the bearer of a message, and of a message, moreover, with which he had been inspired from above, like St Matthew in his painting. In de Decker's words: they knew that with Rembrandt it was not a matter of 'ingeniousness' but a matter of the 'Scriptures', that is, the revelation of God.

It is important for us to know this circle, for in some of their writings a kind of independent commentary may be found to Rembrandt's biblical works. Of course this commentary is not equal to the work. Dullaert and de Decker wrote lines which get very near to Rembrandt's 'matter'. But on the whole there is a great distance between Rembrandt, with his wide and deep vision, and these men whose horizon was more limited. We can only say that in this circle we find a reflection of the spirit which animated Rembrandt's work.

Finally, one more important, negative, conclusion may be drawn: that there is no representative of spiritualist mysticism to be found in Rembrandt's circle. The great wave of 'enthusiastic' piety reached Amsterdam only around the time of Rembrandt's death. The community of Jean de Labadie and Anna Maria van Schurman was founded in Amsterdam in 1669. The circle round Johannes Gichtel who preached Jakob Boehme's mysticism appeared around 1670. With the help of the mayor of Beuningen, Gichtel published Boehme's works in 1682 and 1683. Antoinette Bourignon brought her visionary religiosity to Amsterdam in 1668. Her book *La lumière née en ténèbres* was printed there in 1668. Jan Luyken's book *Jesus and the Soul*, which was wholly inspired by Boehme's mysticism, made spiritualism widely known from 1678. All these movements which according to Labadie put more trust in the Holy Ghost who is still speaking to men, than in the pen of His writers, exercised their vigorous and explosive influence only after Rembrandt's death.

But even in Rembrandt's time the precursors of these new currents were at work in Amsterdam.[102] A number of Jakob Boehme's writings were translated and printed between 1634 and 1644. Petrus Serrarius who called himself a 'preacher of the Catholic Church' and taught that all churches were corrupt and that only

the millennium could now be expected, had, in 1659,
re-introduced the spiritualist mysticism of Entfelder.
Christian Hoburg, whose attitude was equally anti-
church and enthusiastic, had his *Theologia Mystica*
printed in 1655. The circle round the poet and innkeeper
Jan Soet criticized the churches most severely, and
believed that the Second Coming was at hand. The
great Comenius, though not spiritualist in his theological attitude, published the strange *Revelations* by
Dabricius, Cotter and Poniatovski between 1657 and
1665. And in the 'Lambs' War' which broke out among
the Mennonites in 1663, in which Galenus Abrahamsz
played the main part, one of the points was the contrast between the visible and the invisible Church, and
here Galenus came very close to the spiritualist
mysticism of Sebastian Franck.[103]

None of the men whom we find in Rembrandt's
immediate circle belonged to these enthusiastic movements. Dullaert was on friendly terms with Joachim
Oudaen, to whom all churches were the great whore
of St John's Revelation; but as an elder of the Walloon
Church, Dullaert remained a man of the Church.
Heyblocq received in his home the anti-church poet
Jan Soet, who expected the millenium before his
death; but his chief friends were his theological
colleagues like Samuel Maresius, who in the name of
Reformed theology attacked chiliasm. And Heyblocq
himself was true to the line of church orthodoxy. In
this field, Rembrandt had had a painful experience.
The Jewish scholar Menasseh ben Israel had asked
him to illustrate his book *Piedra Gloriosa*. This was a
Messianic exegesis of the dream of Nebuchadnezzar,
where the stones mentioned in the stories of David and

Goliath, Jacob and Nebuchadnezzar are given fanciful identifications. The etchings show that Rembrandt did not find it easy to follow Menasseh's thoughts. He changed the plate again and again.[104] Rembrandt was probably too sober, and had not enough interest in a purely speculative exegesis of the Bible, to feel happy with this work. Obermüller says rightly: 'His humour keeps him down to earth.'[105]

In the whole circle round Rembrandt as well as in Rembrandt's work there is no trace of a mystic religiosity, in which men are engulfed in a universal ground, or in ecstatic experience. Speculations on the function of light in Rembrandt's painting, and the theme of light in mysticism, cannot change the fact that man as represented by Rembrandt always remains an earthly creature who knows about the distance between God and man. The same is true of the men who were his friends. While to the typical mystic, 'the historical person of Christ recedes entirely into the background',[106] to them the Christ of the New Testament is the very centre of history.

Among Rembrandt's acquaintances there are several who may in a certain sense be called pietists. As we have seen, they were in the first place not concerned with dogma and creed, but with their personal life of faith. But this pietism has to be sharply distinguished from the currents of spiritualism which were to be of wide influence after 1670.

This older pietism, which arose in England, exercised an influence in the Netherlands not only in theology[107] but also and especially in literature. Cats and Huygens delighted in the writings of Joseph Hall.[108] Volkerus van Oosterwijck, parson and poet in Delft, with whom de Decker was on friendly terms,[109] and François van Hoogstraten, the friend of Dullaert,[110] translated some of Hall's works. This pietist theology is anti-scholastic. Hall asks, 'How many things are necessary to a Christian?' and answers, 'Two: knowledge and practice.' On his view the danger of the sixteenth century had been ignorance, whereas in the seventeenth century it was trying to know too much. Hence at the Synod of Dordrecht he preached about a text certainly not expected by the assembly: 'Be not righteous over much; neither make thyself over wise' (Eccl. 7.16).[111] Amesius, who imported Puritanism from England to Holland and who became a professor in Franeker, said: '*Theologia est doctrina Deo vivendi.*' But this pietism is not spiritualistic in the sense of mysticism. Salvation is brought about through the Word of the Revelation, and what we find here is no more than a protest against intellectualist orthodoxy, and the demand for a personal share in the event announced to us in the Scriptures. For the spiritualists, however, the direct 'revelations' stand beside the Scriptures, or even replace them. For them, the 'inner logos' is of importance, not the 'external' one. Gichtel wants to have 'the spirit of God preach within himself'. In their teaching, the idea of rebirth is more important than the biblical story of salvation. According to Jan Luyken's words taken over from Boehme 'the Son of the historical records remains a stranger'.[112] This leads to detailed descriptions of the different conditions of the soul, and thus again the stress is shifted away from the objective historical event towards the subjective experience of man.

In the circle of Rembrandt's friends we find neither

this 'enthusiastic' spiritualism nor this self-observation. There we do not hear that the old dogma of predestination is opposed in the name of a new dogma of re-born man, nor that the Holy Spirit is detached from the Scriptures.

Another characteristic of the Spiritualists is that they call in question the Church itself,[113] which for them is the 'Babel of the external Church'. This too is far from being the attitude of any friends of Rembrandt. Though these men could speak very critically of the Church, they did not dream of disavowing it.

Paul Hazard has described the great crisis of the European mind[114] which, between 1680 and 1715, shook everything, and was felt in Holland too; we may even say that in the Netherlands, which have always been open to so many intellectual movements, it began earlier, and its first effects were felt in Amsterdam in the fifties and sixties. One of the characteristic symptoms of this crisis is a turning from the objective to the subjective, from theocentric to anthropocentric thought. Although Rembrandt does not seem to have been intimately associated with the typical representatives of this new current, he may have felt that a great change was coming. But he had chosen his way. For him it is clear that man stands in the great context in which he is placed by God. He knows that what counts is not man by himself, nor the piety of man, but the history of God's dealings with man. Thus we may say of him, what Conrad Ferdinand Meyer says of Luther:

> *He feels the great upheaval of the age,*
> *And firmly clasps his Bible.*

CHAPTER NINE

Rembrandt's Message

★ ★ ★

THE question as to the true inner content of Rembrandt's work has been answered in many different ways.

Jakob Burckhardt, the loyal partisan of the Renaissance, declares that Rembrandt has been concerned with the Bible story less for reasons of devotion than because it was the popular theme which was intelligible to all. He refuses to discover a 'biblical feeling' in his work.[1]

Georg Simmel sees in him the perfect example of religious man who can do without transcendental realities, because for him religion consists rather in a temper of the soul than in the affirmation of a revealed truth.[2]

Carl Neumann regards the artist as a great mystic of the same kind as Jakob Boehme. Everything is dominated by the mystical feeling that all things of the body are only a disguise of the divine powers, that God's nearness may be felt everywhere, and that light is its messenger.[3]

For Eugène Fromentin the painter is a spiritualist, an ideologist, a mind which is only concerned with pure ideas.[4]

As regards the denominational character of his work, Wilhelm Hausenstein thinks it is more Roman Catholic than Protestant, for, he says, there is something of the childlike simplicity of the Middle Ages in Rembrandt, and his mysticism is inconsistent with Protestantism.[5]

Van Ryckevorsel believes it impossible to conclude from Rembrandt's works what his denomination was. He refuses to find in them any characteristic signs of Protestant piety.[6]

In contrast to this W. Martin recognizes in Rembrandt the first painter to have broken with the traditional views and to have attempted a Protestant exegesis of the Bible.[7]

The basic features of Rembrandt's art, Werner Weisbach writes, connect him with Protestantism and place him in opposition to the Counter-Reformation. For the artist refused to deify outward forms. Like Luther, he emphasized the humiliation of Jesus Christ and thus opposed the heroic conceptions of the Counter-Reformation. His faith was quite subjective, without any dogmatic pattern. Hence, Rembrandt may be compared to Kierkegaard.[8]

Wilhelm Bode sees the most exalted expression of Dutch Calvinism in the work of this great painter.[9] Emile Doumergue goes even further and discovers, in Rembrandt's work, the application of Calvinist teaching to the field of art.[10] Léon Wencelius tries to prove a close connection between Calvin and Rembrandt.[11]

A. M. Hind thinks Rembrandt is to be classified outside Calvinism, because, in his opinion, the emphasis is laid more on the love of God than on his justice.[12]

C. Vosmaer states that the supernatural has little attraction for him, and that he 'humanized' the Bible.[13]

Rembrandt was no Calvinist, no champion of any

community of believers, nor supporter of any sect, writes Schmidt Degener. He kept aloof from any dogmatism. But he can see in Rembrandt a mild Pauline Christianity and a certain rationalism. He believes that Rembrandt is the only artist to have rendered the genuine temper of the gospel correctly.[14]

In his treatise on Rembrandt's relation to the religious lay movements of his time, Hans Martin Rotermund comes to the conclusion that in the middle of the forties, Rembrandt was deeply affected by the outlook of the *Doopsgezinden* (Mennonites) and that this conditioned his attitude as a Christian.[15]

The enumeration of all these opinions may be concluded by a saying of François Mauriac: 'It seems to me that Rembrandt has given the most faithful representation of the Bible stories.'[16]

What are we to think of so many contradictory opinions? Must we be content with the statement that the one is as good as the other? Some of the above opinions come from art historians who are more competent in the field of art criticism than in that of cultural and church history. Others, however, emphasize important aspects of the master's religious artistic creation which must not be overlooked.

We have seen that an investigation into Rembrandt's relation with the Church does not lead to any definite conclusions. But with the help of his biblical works and the remarks of those near to him we may form a judgment on his inner attitude which is more than a purely subjective impression. The most definite fact is that Rembrandt *lived* with his Bible. During the first half of his life the Bible was no more than a rich source for his artistic imagination. But in the course of time it revealed itself to him as the eternal truth; he listened to it, and he interpreted it. This inner development contributed to the creation of a personal style appropriate to the biblical language. From then on he employed an indirect and severely restrained form of expression. It was adapted to the mystery of that revelation whose contents are not the glorification of man, but the act of God descending to man.

What place must be given to Rembrandt within the history of religious art? A retrospective glance at the main epochs of that history will help us to answer this question.

At the beginning of the Middle Ages, Christian art was fully turned towards transcendental realities. The Byzantine painters lived in an objective, supernatural and sanctified world. The Bible story was detached from this life and entirely enacted in the 'other world'. And even when nature reclaimed its place and the Franciscan movement tried to give to piety a human touch and a personal note, this natural and human element was set in the frame-work of a higher world far beyond the reach of earthly reality. This is still true of Fra Angelico and Memling whose pictures take us 'into a kind of religious contemplation of an ideal stillness and seclusion, where all passions cease, all discord ends, where there is prayer and adoration, where everything is transfigured.'[17]

But even as early as the Middle Ages, another spirit began to stir. Biblical events were gradually reinstated in this world, quite naïvely at first, but afterwards quite deliberately. Hallowed things became more intimate. But along with this, the danger arose of Christian and profane or pagan motives merging into one another in a general way. In the art of the Renaissance, the biblical God was mixed with the gods and heroes of Olympus, and the interspersing of biblical subjects with mythological themes of the classical age was soon an accomplished fact. Thus we can only with difficulty distinguish the predominant tendency of these painters: Is it to merge the eternal into daily life, or to exploit religious subjects for purely aesthetic purposes? The ideal of the beauty of form prevailed in the end. Raphael expects us to admire the human body, the harmony of lines and colours, but he by no means demands the affirmation of our faith. At the sight of his *Transfiguration*, Taine had to ask the question: 'In this miracle of his, does Raphael believe in anything at all?' and he answers: 'He believes above all that the accurate choice and arrangement of the figures is supremely important.'[18]

The Roman Catholic Church, which had been warned by the Reformation of the pagan spirit spreading in art saw the danger. The Council of Trent forbade 'the setting up in churches of pictures influenced by erroneous doctrine leading the simple-minded astray.'[19] Was a return, then, intended to the supernatural, ritualistic representations of the early Middle Ages? No, for the Church needed an art which aimed at conquest, and could support it in its fight against the Protestants and the indifferent. A dynamic gift of persuasion was more important than the peaceful pursuit of meditation. Moreover, it would have been a hopeless enterprise to root out from the Church the predilection for wholly worldly classical art, and for worldly things altogether. Thus religious art had to find a synthesis between the Renaissance beauty of form and the requirements of church strategy. Out of this was born baroque art, the style of the Counter-Reformation, whose basic features are defined by Louis Gillet as follows: 'The Counter-Reformation succeeded in finding a common denominator for classical life and Christianity, reason and emotion, nature and faith, legend and gospel. . . . This liberal world of human ideas, in which Plato and Augustine, the Bible and Virgil, natural and divine inspiration have equal shares, this ingenious compromise between the two parts of our double inheritance, devised by the classical mind, was certainly a masterpiece of culture. Have we to be reminded that it was a product of the Church?'[20] Striking though this description may be, it is incomplete, for baroque art comprises a *third* factor: the new spirit of a Roman Catholicism whose law had ceased to be generally recognized, which had to fight for its existence and looked around for weapons for the great counter-attack it was about to launch. These weapons were to be furnished by the religious psychology of the Jesuits, which applies itself to the feeling and at the same time seeks to satisfy the wants of modern man. From now on, religious art was essentially this-worldly. It tried to express the holy by an analogy of being, that is to say by raising and glorifying human qualities, so that the difference between the eternal and the temporal is more quantitative rather than qualitative. In this respect, Eugénio d'Ors'[21] definition of baroque art as the 'style of continuity', expressing the 'naturalness of the supernatural', contains a great deal of truth. 'Soaring forms', 'canonization of movement', a gaze uplifted to heaven, and unsteady, bombastic language are the expression of this romantic religious feeling which attempts to ascend upwards to God, without that peaceful certainty which arises from faith in the God who comes down to man.

Baroque art needs obvious means of persuasion: here Christ is a superman, the Virgin a victorious queen, and the saints are heroes. Even in the representation of suffering, it tries to arouse our admiration. It is the avowed style of glorification, and thus it glorifies Christ, Mary, the saints, and above all the Church, which is made into a spiritual and secular great power, into 'a kind of demi-god who has taken the place of the true God and has been supplied with all his prerogatives'.[22] From now on Roman Catholic art (and a great deal of Protestant art too) almost without exception proclaimed a gospel whose centre was the believer, and in which the glory that is to come had been anticipated.

What place did Rembrandt take in this historical development? As we saw, at the beginning of his career he largely succumbed to the influence of contemporary religious painting. For several years he allowed himself to be impressed by the force and majesty of baroque art, without however attaining a harmonious synthesis between the spirit of the Bible and the rhetorical language of the baroque style. He lived with a compromise, and we are almost inclined to believe that he did not himself believe in his own means of expression. Did he not feel too deeply stirred by this simplicity of the Bible to follow that pompous and boastful fashion?

There came a time when he discovered how impossible it was to represent in this way what he found in the Bible. He broke free from the pressure of the *Zeitgeist* and created a personal style of his own. This style is full of tension, for it has to proclaim the most contradictory of all messages: God the Lord becomes 'as any other man'. These joyful tidings demand close contact with the worldly things of this life, but at the same time they must proclaim this God who intervenes in the destinies of mankind, as the Lord of heaven and earth. Divine transcendence breaking into human life in this world must be shown, and yet the relation with concrete worldly reality must be maintained. In forcing the ineffable into human forms, Rembrandt shows that the mystery of Revelation does not consist in the glorification of man, but in the complete abasement of God. The entire biblical story is meant to lead us to the cross: here, it is not the first word which is given to the glory, but the very last. The majesty of God and his Son, which remains hidden to the world, is only revealed to faith.

Therefore it is rather with great reticence than with grand, pathetic gestures, rather through suffering than through glory, rather in quietude than in movement, that we shall penetrate to the divine mystery. The desire to embellish the gospel for apologetic reasons contradicts the biblical truth, and can only result in less being said than the Holy Scriptures themselves do in all their simplicity.

Luther makes an unambiguous distinction between a theology of glory and the true theology of the cross. The theology of glory, he says, 'prefers works to suffering, glory to the cross, power to weakness, wisdom to foolishness, and in one word evil to good'. But the theology of the cross knows that 'it is not enough for anybody nor does it help him that he recognizes God in his glory and majesty, unless he recognizes him in the abasement and ignominy of the cross'.[23] In analogy to this we may describe Rembrandt's style as a 'painting of the cross'.

In this sense only is it possible to speak of Rembrandt's Protestantism. He was Protestant, because he became more and more deeply absorbed in the biblical testimony, because he interpreted the gospel in the light only of this very gospel, without calling in the assistance of any classical or humanist ideal, and because he did not attempt to force the paradox of the cross into human dimensions.[24]

And yet his art cannot really be classified in any system. It is too personal for that. Nor has it produced a school. The fact that Rembrandt in the second half of his life—consciously or unconsciously—protested against the official Roman Catholic art of his time, does not mean that his style can be termed a 'Protestant' or a 'Calvinist' style. Such an expression would only have a meaning if this style had been accepted by the Protestant churches. But Protestantism has shown little interest in his work and has received baroque art with open arms. It has not been at all aware of the basic contradiction between this art and foundations of its own faith.

Thus Rembrandt is the painter whose art seeks to express a faith exclusively rooted in the gospel. His message may be summarized in the words of Ecclesiastes: 'I know that, whatsoever God doeth, it shall be for ever: nothing can be put to it, nor any thing taken from it: and God hath done it, that men should fear before him.'

Notes

References to paintings are from *Rembrandt's Paintings,* Bredius (Phaidon).

References to drawings are from *Rembrandts Handzeichnungen,* Valentiner (Klassiker der Kunst).

References to etchings are from Bartsch's catalogue.

* This sign refers to the reproductions in this book.

CHAPTER ONE

1. A. M. Hind, *Summary List of Drawings and Etchings by Rembrandt,* British Museum.

2. 'Liveliness', and not 'movement', cp. J. C. van Gelder, *Rembrandt's Vroegste Ontwikkeling,* 1953, p. 297. Grotius praises the *beweeglijkheit* in a tragedy by Vondel. (Brandt, *Leven van Vondel,* ed. Verwijs, p. 58.)

3. Painting in Dresden, cf. Huizinga's judgment, in *Holländische Kultur des siebzehnten Jahrhunderts,* p. 50.

4. Schmidt Degener, in the *Catalogue of the Exhibition of Biblical Art,* Amsterdam, 1939.

5. The document of 1671 published by Bredius in *Oud Holland,* 1909, p. 238ff.

CHAPTER TWO

1. Van Hoogstraten, Document No. 341 (Hofstede de Groot, *Documents on Rembrandt*).

2. Schmidt Degener, Preface to the *Catalogue of the Exhibition of Biblical Art,* Amsterdam, 1939. Cp. Busken Huet, *Het Land van Rembrandt* II, 3, 164.

3. Neumann, *Rembrandt,* Berlin 1905, p. 599.

4. Emile Mâle, *L'art religieux après le Concile de Trente,* p. 17.

5. Large edition of the Rembrandt Bible by Hofstede de Groot, 1906. Small edition by E. W. Bredt, 1921.

6. It is specially interesting to note that Rembrandt never treated the great theme of the artists of the Counter-Reformation, The Repentence of St Mary Magdalen, 'which has been represented by painters a hundred times' (Emile Mâle). He does not even give a single exegesis of the proper text on which the tradition of Mary Magdalene is based (the seventh chapter of St Luke).

7. 'Rembrandt and the Religious Lay Movements in the Netherlands of his Time' in *Nederlandsch Kunsthistorisch Jaarboek,* 1953.

8. It is certain that this is meant to be St Paul because, just as in the other paintings of St Paul, his attributes of book and sword are to be seen (*Bredius*, 601, 602 and 612). But it is uncertain whether this picture is one of a series representing the apostles.

The two other paintings of the later years which represent St Paul are *Bredius* numbers 612 and 297. Concerning the last-named see Knuttel, *Rembrandt*, p. 193 for the reasons why this must be considered a representation of St Paul.

9. See Chapter Four.

10. See Chapter Three.

11. Confession of Lubbert Gerrits and Hans de Ries (10 and 11). Cf. Wenger, *Glimpses of Mennonite Doctrine and History*, p. 162.

12. It is odd to note that the great poet Vondel, in his Mennonite period, compared the deliverance of the children of Israel with the liberation of the Dutch people (Busken Huet, *Het Land van Rembrandt*, 2, 1, 115).

13. 'Rembrandt's Werk und das Problem der christlichen Kunst' in the *Monatsschrift für Gottesdienst und kirchliche Kunst*, 1933, 1.

14. Rohault de Fleury, 'L'Evangile'. *Etudes Iconographiques*, II, 291.

15. Confession of Lubbert Gerrits and Hans de Ries: Art. 32. Confession of Dordrecht: Art. 10.

16. Meihuizen, *Galenus Abrahamsz*, Haarlem 1954, p. 60.

17. The Washing of the Feet which played a special part among the Mennonites, was depicted by Rembrandt only three, perhaps four times.

18. Edition of 1639.

19. A painting of 1646 is missing (Document 107).

20. With Calvin already, then in the Dutch Creed, in the Heidelberg Catechism and in the Reformed Liturgy of Baptism.

21. Jan Engelman in *Nederlandsche Schilderkunst in Beeld*, p. 26.

CHAPTER THREE

1. Eugene Fromentin, *Les maîtres d'autrefois*, p. 34.

2. Calvin, *Commentary* on I Tim. 3.16.

3. C. J. Holmes, *Notes on the Art of Rembrandt*, p. 36.

4. *Table Talks* in Helbig, Martin Luther, *Theologie des Kreuzes*, Kröner, p. 119.

5. In Phil. 2.7.

6. Ed. Brunschvigg, p. 214.

7. An explanation of the anagram was first given by Bojanovski and accepted by J. H. Scholte (*Nieuwe Rotterdamsche Courant*, 24th March 1940). H. M. Rotermund comes to the same conclusion in his essay in *Die Sammlung* (June 1954). In all likeli-

hood we may regard the etching as a rejection of alchemy. Similarly, de Decker wrote against alchemy in his *Praise of Avarice* and his *Puntdicht* against astrology: 'that my signs of the zodiac may be the line of the apostles, and my sunlight, Christ.' (*Rijmoeffeningen*, Tweede Boeck, p. 5).

8. See further under Chapter Five, The Miracle of Christmas.

9. *Notes on the Art of Rembrandt*, p. 112.

10. Georg Simmel, *Rembrandt*, Leipzig 1917, p. 159.

11. Matt. 7.29.

12. Hans Martin Rotermund, *Rembrandt und die religiösen Laienbewegungen*, p. 154.

13. Rotermund writes that in the Reformed Church one could not describe Christ in a picture apprehensible to the senses (p. 148). This gives quite a wrong impression of Reformed piety in the seventeenth century. In fact the concrete descriptions sometimes went too far. As examples, I may quote Voetius' edition of Bayly's *Oeffeninge der Godsaligheydt* (1642), pp. 494ff., Heinsius, *Lofsanck van Jesus Christus* (1616), and Revius' *Godsgeschiedenis* (1630). One can hardly go further in visualizing the life and suffering of Christ than these men do.

14. 'The Motif of Radiance in Rembrandt's Biblical Drawings', *Journal of the Courtauld Institutes and Warburg*, Nos. 3 and 4, 1952.

15. The only exception is probably the *Emmaus* drawing of 1629 (Cat. 525).

CHAPTER FOUR

1. For this, see mainly: Van Rijckevorsel, *Rembrandt en de Traditie*, Rotterdam.

2. Valentiner No. 322.

3. Cp. Mâle, *L'art religieux depuis le Concile de Trente*, p. 360.

4. Weisbach, *Rembrandt*, p. 209.

5. B. 61.

6. Weisbach, *Der Barock als Kunst der Gegenreformation*, p. 93.

7. Document 346.

8. Valentiner No. 552.

9. Emile Mâle, *op. cit.*, p. 30.

10. Luther, *Selected Works*, Calwer, p. 90.

11. Calvin, *Commentary* on St Luke 1, 48.

12. See below: Joseph's Dream.

13. Luther, *op. cit.*, p. 91.

14. In Dutch *nederheyt*; Luther *Niedrigkeit*; Calvin *petitesse*, whereas the Vulgate has *humilitas*. The marginal comment of the Reformed synodal version says: 'the lowly situation; for it is not in keeping with the virtue of humility to boast of humility'.

15. Mâle, *op. cit.*, p. 30.

16. Hans Martin Rotermund, *Rembrandt und die religiösen Laienbewegungen in den Niederlanden seiner Zeit*, p. 161.

17. W. A. P. Smit, *De Dichter Revius*, p. 159.

18. *Eerste Boeck der Rijm-Oeffeningen*, 1659, p. 75. Cf. *Tweede Boeck der Puntdichten*, p. 160: *O suyvre Moedermaegd, te recht hebt ghij verkregen den naam van Segenrijck.*

CHAPTER FIVE

1. B. 45.

2. Quotation of 1776 at Münz, *Die Kunst Rembrandts und Goethes Sehen*, Leipzig 1934, p. 94. Later in Goethe's life, the Italian masters triumphed after all. During his Italian journey he wrote that 'the purity of form and its distinctness' are more interesting than the 'vigorous crudeness and floating spirituality' of Rembrandt.

3. Burckhardt, *Kulturgeschichtliche Vorträge*, Leipzig, p. 124.

4. E. Mâle, *L'art religieux après le Concile de Trente*, p. 314.

CHAPTER SIX

1. Rembrandt's contemporaries who were better acquainted with the Bible than their descendants, recognized all the details of St Matthew's chapter in this picture, as is proved by a poem of H. F. Waterloos which is written on the copy of the National Library in Paris (Document 266). See p. 64.

CHAPTER SEVEN

1. Hans Martin Rotermund makes this remark in his essay on *Rembrandt und die religiösen Laienbewegungen in den Niederlanden seiner Zeit*. I owe much to this study. But Rotermund has quite a wrong conception of Reformed piety in the seventeenth century and quotes as Mennonite much that can be found in Reformed circles too.

2. It is strange that none of the many Mennonites and Collegiants who played a part in the conflicts around Galenus Abrahamsz (in Amsterdam from 1646) is ever mentioned in connection with Rembrandt (cf. H. W. Meihuizen's *Galenus Abrahamsz* (1954) where these struggles are described in detail). The fact that Rembrandt painted the wife of a Mennonite preacher with Collegiant tendencies (Catherina Hooghsaet in 1657) is of course not sufficient proof of closer relations with this circle.

3. Brandt, *Historie der Reformatie*, III, 639.

4. Document 37 and Vosmaer, *Rembrandt*, p. 129.

5. A. Kuyper, *Johannes Maccovius*, 1899.

6. Hales and Balcanqual, *Korte Historie van het Synode van Dordrecht 1671*, pp. 354 and 373.

7. Kuyper, *Johannes Maccovius*, pp. 153, 159 and 253. His main writing against the Baptists is *Proton Pseudos Anabaptistarum.* Cocceius compares him to a dog who dutifully barks at the enemies, but goes on barking even when he deals with innocent people (cf. Bayle, *Dictionnaire, in voce,* Makovski).

8. Documents 34, 43 and 60. Cf. *Catalogue of the Rembrandthuis 1925,* p. 37.

9. B. 266. According to the *Catalogue of the Rembrandthuis* the drawing in Berlin (Val. 275) represents Sylvius baptizing Rembrandt's little daughter Cornelia. In Valentiner's opinion, this claim is without foundation. Benesch sees in the drawing a preliminary study for the *Baptist's Sermon* in Berlin. But the figures of the drawing cannot be found there. The old man has nothing to do with the Baptist and greatly resembles Sylvius whom we know from the etchings. The date of the drawing given by Benesch (1638) corresponds exactly to the one of Cornelia's baptism (November 1638).

10. Bredius 237.

11. B. 280.

12. Documents 43, 60, 78, 89.

13. Huizinga, *Nederland's Beschaving in de zeventiende eeuw,* p. 82.

14. Bredius 173.

15. B. 279.

16. Bredius 213.

17. Brandt, *Historie der Reformatie,* III, 810.

18. Not from 1648 to 1656, as I wrote in *Rembrandt et la Bible,* Neuchâtel 1947, on the strength of Hofstede de Groot's statements. See the article on Keihl in Thieme-Becker.

19. Valentiner 724 and 725.

20. B. 271.

21. Bredius 409. To me it seems unlikely that the woman is really Anslo's wife. Anslo's whole attitude rather suggests that he is engaged in a pastoral talk with a woman of his congregation.

22. No excommunication without previous warning (Matt. 18.15-18).

23. The most important period for relations between Mennonites and Socinians was the period of disputes, in which Galenus Abrahamsz played the main part, i.e. after 1655. But that was the time when Rembrandt, as we see, associated with a small circle of friends whose Christian belief was opposed to rationalism.

24. In the early forties, Samuel van Hoogstraten was Rembrandt's pupil. He came from a Mennonite family and may have made Rembrandt acquainted with other Mennonites. But van Hoogstraten was not a very zealous Mennonite. In 1648 he was

admonished by the congregation in Dordrecht, 'because he carried a sword', and in 1656 he was excommunicated for his marriage with a woman who did not belong to the congregation, and for other reasons not specially indicated. He then became a member of the Reformed Church. The biographical notes he wrote on Rembrandt do not give us the impression that he understood the deeper intentions of his master (cf. Vosmaer, *Rembrandt*, Second Edition, 1877, p. 238).

25. Hans Martin Rotermund, *op. cit.*, p. 189.

26. Here we have not to do with the ban, i.e. a public excommunication, but with 'suspension' from the communion until the person concerned has shown true repentance and an amendment of his ways (cf. Niesel, *Bekenntnisschriften und Kirchenordnungen der nach Gottes Wort reformierten Kirche*, pp. 281 and 323, and *Church Ordinance, Dordrecht 1618-1619*, Art. 76).

27. Wijnman's article in *Amstelodanum* (June 1956) has convinced me that Cornelia was born in 1654 rather than in 1651 or 1652. The evidence is contradictory, but the most important document is certainly the record concerning the disciplinary case of 1654.

28. Schotel-Rogge, *De openbare Eeredienst der N.H. Kerk*, p. 368.

29. Cf. S. D. van Veen, *Kerkelijk Opzicht en Tucht, 1910*, pp. 10 and 23, and Cramer, *De Theologische Faculteit te Utrecht ten tijde van Voetius*, p. 427, and Schotel Rogge, p. 368.

30. With regard to this, Rotermund comes to the same conclusion (*op. cit.*, pp. 185-6).

31. It does strike us as peculiar that the man who was such a great collector, possessed practically no books at all (as both inventories prove).

CHAPTER EIGHT

1. *Der Alte Rembrandt*, p. 1.

2. Document 407. Sandrat speaks of 'lowly people' (Document 329).

3. After 1654 we hear no more of Jan Six. Menasseh ben Israel had left for England in 1655, and we do not know if Rembrandt became specially friendly with other members of the Jewish community. I shall not mention Jan Vos since he belonged to the 'official' set (as Schmidt Degener shows, *op. cit.*, p. 16). The only poem in which he speaks about Rembrandt in a personal way was probably written in 1654. It is uncertain whether Ph. de Koning was connected with Rembrandt in those years. According to Valentiner (*Handzeichnungen*, II, XXII), S. van Hoogstraten is also believed to have remained in touch with Rembrandt in the later years. From what he has written

about his master, we cannot gather that he was very close to him.

4. Gersaint, *Catalogue Raisonné*, 1751, p. 199.

5. B. 273.

6. 3rd May 1633. (Information from the archives of the congregation, Amsterdam.)

7. Document 317.

8. Information from Professor M. van Rhijn, Utrecht.

9. Detailed information on the Dusart family in Bredius' *Artists' Inventories*. Christiaen died in 1682.

10. Among them, portraits of the Reformed pastor Rulitius and the Lutheran pastor Visscher.

11. Document 306.

12. J. de Vries, *Jeremias de Decker*, 1807, p. 106.

13. *Derde Boeck der Rijm-Oeffeningen*, p. 141.

14. The poems printed in *Rijm-Oeffeningen*, in which Oudaen, Glasius and Waterloos express their admiration for de Decker, show that *Good Friday* was looked upon as his most important work.

15. Preface to the first book of the *Puntdichten*.

16. *Tweede Boeck des Vervolgs*, p. 41.

17. He himself speaks too modestly of his style which 'creeps along the ground' (Third book, p. 160).

18. *Eerste Boeck des Vervolgs*, p. 16.

19. Langhelius was one of the leading ministers of religion in Amsterdam and played a great part in the struggle of the Church against the performance of Vondel's *Lucifer* and against the 'heresies' of the Collegiants.

20. De Decker gives a detailed description of his attitude towards the Church in his letters to Westerbaen (In de Vries, *Jeremias de Decker*, 1807).

21. 'Merx Tartarea' in *Derde Boeck*, p. 45.

22. The first portrait, which Waterloos praises in a poem printed in 1660, is missing. The second is Br 320 (of 1666). De Raaf's suggestion that he only painted one portrait, which remained unfinished for more than six years, does not carry conviction (*Oud Holland*, 1912).

23. Document 291.

24. Here we find Schmidt Degener's interpretation of the Phoenix etching confirmed. In this poem, we find the same contrast between fame and envy (Schmidt Degener, *Rembrandt*, 1954, p. 128).

25. Among other poems on the pastors who protested against Vondel's biblical dramas.

26. Document 221.

27. Document 222.

28. See Schotel-Rogge: '*De Openbare Eeredienst*, second edition p. 368. Cramer, *De theologische faculteit te Utrecht ten tijde van Voetius*, p. 427, gives the text of a report of the theological faculty of Utrecht which shows that in such cases exhortation by the Church Council without public confession is considered a very moderate form of discipline.

29. *Album Amicorum*, p. 222.

30. Valentiner 318.

31. The only other drawing in the *Album*, which is accompanied by a poem in a similar way, is the one by Jan van der Cappelle.

32. Document 262.

33. Document 416.

34. Valentiner 415.

35. As Benesch does in *Rembrandts Vermächtnis*. On the other hand, cf. Martin: 'He was one of the few pupils who understood Rembrandt.' (*De Hollandsche Schilderkunst in de 17de eeuw*, p. 130.) According to Thieme Becker, he was Rembrandt's favourite pupil.

36. F. Lugt in *Inventaire général des dessins des Ecoles du Nord, Ecole hollandaise*, Tome III, Musée du Louvre, p. 40.

37. The question is whether Jan van der Cappelle should not be named here too. But I see no proof that he was in personal touch with Rembrandt in later years. In the Heyblocq Album he appears in 1654. He had a magnificent collection of Rembrandt's drawings, which, however, does not necessarily imply that this wealthy 'industrialist' was on friendly personal terms with Rembrandt.

38. Cf. document 428. Rembrandt painted him too. (Br 311 in 1662; cf. Catalogue, Rembrandt Exhibition, Amsterdam 1932). One feels that he liked this young man with his smiling eyes.

39. Lilienfeld, *Arent de Gelder*, 1914. The self-portrait is in Leningrad.

40. Dr J. Wille, *Heiman Dullaert*, pp. 40 and 158.

41. Frans Bastiaanse, *Nederlandsche Letterkunde*, II, 222.

42. Dr J. Wille, *Heiman Dullaert*, p. 158. The etching is B. 96 of 1645.

43. *Op. cit.*, p. 163.

44. He also translated a book by Jean Puget de la Serre, *Onderhoud der goede geesten op de ijdelheden der wereld* and a book by the pastor de Rochefort on the West Indies.

45. *Réponse de Charles Drélincourt à la lettre écrite par Monseigneur le prince Ernest, Landgrave de Hesse aux cinq ministres de Paris*. Second edition, Geneva 1664, p. 237.

46. *Op. cit.*, p. 421.

47. First editions 1657 in London and Sédan. From 1680 to 1740 six editions of Dullaert's translation appeared.

48. *Dictionnaire*, III, 773.

49. Edition Genève, 1729, Livre II, Chap. 18.

50. V. 7.

51. B. 276.

52. *Exhibition of Biblical Art*, Amsterdam, p. 29.

53. According to F. Lugt, Br 326 (painted in 1667) is a portrait of Lutma Junior.

54. Bredius in *Oud Holland*, 1912, pp. 219ff.

55. Bredius, *Artists' Inventories*, I, 96.

56. Mr H. F. Wijnman, 'Mr Lieven van Coppenol' in *Yearbook Amstelodamum*, 1933.

57. Wijnman, *op. cit.*, p. 130.

58. It is better, therefore, not to quote the Coppenols as an example for Rembrandt's relations with the Mennonites, as does Rotermund (*op. cit.*, p. 188) when mentioning Coppenols wife.

59. Depicted in Wijnman, *op. cit.*

60. Further collaborators are Asselijn, Boogart and van Petersen, who also wrote poems in which Rembrandt is mentioned. Also H. Sweerds, editor of a work by the father of Jeremias de Decker. After this poet's death, the inventory mentions a picture of de Decker painted by Rembrandt. The three ministers of religion were Simonides (Dullaert's friend), Sanderus and à Vliet.

61. Dr J. Wille, *Heiman Dullaert*, pp. 22-37.

62. In October 1660, Huygens was with Heyblocq. Rembrandt's drawing must date from the first months of the year 1661 (Document 240).

63. Neumann, *op. cit.*, pp. 646ff.

64. De Decker, *Eerste Boeck der Puntdichten*, 1659, p. 29.

65. Of the thirteen names mentioned in *Het Gebedt onzes Heeren*, eight are to be found in the Heyblocq Album.

66. In *Rijm-Oeffeningen*, 1659.

67. *Tweede en leste Boeck des Vervolgs der Rijm-Oeffeningen*, p. 90.

68. The poem in which Jan Vos praises the painting (Br 530) *Haman at the meal of Ahasuerus and Esther* (Document 247), rather serves as an example of how a poet, who finds a painter unsympathetic, reads into his picture what he wants to see in it. The point is that the king is not yet 'raging', but that we feel, as Weisbach says, the uncanny silence before the storm breaks.

69. Document 266.

70. The words run: 'Uw' meesterlijcke streken . . . heb ick sien gaen langs dit paneel.'

71. It is not without significance that there is a hand-written copy of de Decker's poem on the back of the painting of 1638 in Buckingham Palace.

72. *Tweede Boeck des Vervolgs der Rijm-Oeffeningen*, 1667, p. 85. First printed in *De Hollandtsche Parnas*, 1660.

73. Valentiner 318.

74. Document 240.

75. Minister in Dordrecht. He wrote *Den Roomschen Uylen-spiegel*, a very sharp and coarse attack upon evil conditions in the Roman Catholic Church.

76. Dordrecht Town Archivist has kindly informed me that in 1661 there was no member of the Lydius family who might be taken into consideration here.

77. He had also written a panegyric poem in *Het Gebedt onzes Heeren*.

78. To Westerbaen (de Vries, *op. cit.*, p. 108). Cf. *Eerste Boeck der Puntdichten*, p. 39.

79. *Eerste Boeck der Puntdichten*, p. 33.

80. *Derde Boeck*, p. 34.

81. *Traité*, edition of 1729, II, 121.

82. In Jacobus Heyblocq's *Album Amicorum*.

83. *Eerste Boeck der Rijm-Oeffeningen*, p. 47.

84. In the Royal Library in The Hague.

85. This pastor Leupenius visited Heyblocq in 1667, along with his son Johannes, who in those years was Rembrandt's pupil. The fact that a well-known minister entrusted his son to Rembrandt, must mean, that in the last years of his life Rembrandt was no longer looked upon by church people as a black sheep.

86. *Derde Boeck*, p. 80.

87. The lines on Hotton's sermon against avarice in *Derde Boeck*, p. 80, go well with the sermon on p. 79 of 'Praise of Avarice'.

88. *De Christiana inter Europaeos Evangelicos sive Tolerantia in Charitate stabilienda*, 1647 (also in French and Dutch).

89. Some of Stella's writings were on the Roman Index.

90. Dr J. Wille, *Heiman Dullaert*, p. 34.

91. *Derde Boeck der Rijm-Oeffeningen*, p. 45.

92. *Ibid.*, p. 37.

93. Farrago Latino-Belgica.

94. *Tweede Boeck der Puntdichten*, p. 147.

95. *Waer in de schrifture selve so sober gaet*, de Vries, *op. cit.*, p. 102.

96. *Rijm-Oeffeningen*, 1659, p. 70.

97. Document 266.

98. Du Moulin, *Traité de la Paix de l'âme* (Ed. de 1729), I, 251.

99. In *Het Gebedt onzes Heeren*; Wille, *Heiman Dullaert*, p. 36.

100. See Schmidt Degener, *Rembrandt und der holländische Barock.*

101. Document 245.

102. Cf. Cornelia W. Roldanus, *Zeventiende Eeuwsche Geestesbloei,* 1938.

103. Meihuizen, *Galenus Abrahamsz,* pp. 58 and 82.

104. F. Landsberger, *Rembrandt, the Jews and the Bible,* 1946, pp. 96ff.

105. Obermüller, *Monatsschrift für Gottesdienst und kirchliche Kunst,* 1933, I.

106. Hylkema, *Reformateurs,* 1902, II, 457, on Gichtel.

107. In 1642 a translation of Lewis Bayly's famous *Practice of Piety* was printed with preface and glossaries by Voetius.

108. Bishop of Norwich. He was one of the representatives of the Church of England at the Synod of Dordrecht.

109. De Decker, *Derde Boeck des Vervolgs,* p. 36 on 'Den Christelijcken Seneca ofte Joseph Hall's 300 goede spreucken', 1657.

110. 'Schoole der Wereld, geopent in 140 vliegende bedenkingen op velerhand gezichten en zaken', 1682.

111. Brandt, *Historie der Reformatie,* III, 60.

112. *Jezus en de Ziel,* edited by Reitsma, p. 70.

113. This becomes very clear in Hylkema, *Reformateurs,* 1902, where a sharp distinction between the two currents is also made (especially in II, 89).

114. *La crise de la conscience européenne,* 1935.

Chapter Nine

1. Burckhardt, *Kulturgeschichtliche Vorträge,* Kröner, Leipzig, pp. 123 and 125.

2. Georg Simmel, *Rembrandt,* Leipzig 1917, pp. 144-51.

3. Neumann, *Rembrandt,* Berlin 1905, p. 603.

4. Fromentin, *Les maîtres d'autrefois,* p. 129.

5. Wilhelm Hausenstein, *Rembrandt,* Stuttgart 1926, pp. 467-8.

6. Van Ryckevorsel, *Rembrandt en de Traditie,* Rotterdam, p. 31.

7. W. Martin, *De Hollandsche Schilderkunst in de 17de eeuw,* Amsterdam 1936, p. 36.

8. Werner Weisbach, *Rembrandt,* Berlin 1926, pp. 493 and 528.

9. Wilhelm Bode, *Rembrandt und seine Zeitgenossen,* Leipzig 1907, p. 11.

10. Emile Doumergue, *Jean Calvin,* VII, p. 546.

11. Leon Wencelius, *Calvin et Rembrandt,* Paris 1937, p. 235.

12. A. M. Hind, *Rembrandt,* London 1938, p. 7.

13. C. Vosmaer, *Rembrandt,* The Hague 1877, p. 419.

14. Schmidt Degener, *Rembrandt und der Holländische Barock,*

Leipzig 1928, pp. 17 and 45. Schmidt Degener, Preface to the Catalogue of the Exhibition of Biblical Art, Amsterdam 1939.

15. Hans-Martin Rotermund, *Rembrandt und die religiösen Laienbewegungen in den Niederlanden seiner Zeit*, p. 189.

16. F. Mauriac in *Le visage du Christ,* Paris 1938, p. 11.

17. Fromentin, *Maîtres d'autrefois*, p. 354.

18. H. Taine, *Voyage en Italie*, I, p. 172.

19. Emile Mâle, *op. cit.,* p. 1.

20. *Nouvelles littéraires*, 21, II, 1936.

21. Eugénio d'Ors, *Du Baroque*, Paris 1935, p. 129.

22. Taine, *op. cit.*, p. 280.

23. *Heidelberger Disputation,* Theses 20 and 21.

24. It is interesting to note that the most important parts of the above conclusions are confirmed by P. R. Regamey, the director of *Art sacré*. In a review of my article in the Roman Catholic journal *Vie intellectuelle* of 25th June 1938 he writes as follows:

'If Rembrandt's religious inspiration is to be expressed in ideas, it can only be formulated like this. If Rembrandt himself did not reflect in such a way, then at least he has experienced it in his painting, and we may make these reflexions in his stead.'

Father Regamey asks further how it is that this Protestant painting does not disturb Roman Catholics, and he decides that Rembrandt has only thrown light on a part of the biblical truth, but that Roman Catholic piety can be fed on that too, as this part does in fact exist, though inseparably joined together with the others. The Roman Catholic 'adjusts' Rembrandt's one-sided attitude, while profiting from his message at the same time.

We are grateful for this understanding, though we question whether Rembrandt's message is properly understood if seen as an elucidation of one 'part' of the gospel only, instead of recognizing it as the very *centre* of the Revelation.

Plates

I

REMBRANDT AND SASKIA
Painting about 1636 (Bredius 30)

Is this real joy, or else 'the lust of the eyes, and the vainglory of life'?

I John 2.16

II

REMBRANDT AS ST. PAUL
Painting of 1661 (Bredius 59)

'For when I am weak, then am I strong.'

II Cor. 12.10

III

ECCE HOMO
Etching of 1636 (Bredius 77)

The Gospel becomes a sentimental melodrama.

IV

ECCE HOMO

Etching of 1655 (Bredius 76)

'Behold, the man!' At the sight of him everybody must ask himself: 'What then shall I do
unto Jesus which is called Christ?'

Matt. 27.22

V

THE RAISING OF LAZARUS

Etching about 1632 (Bredius 73)

Rembrandt only sees the physical miracle which he stresses by Jesus' theatrical attitude and the terrified gestures of the spectators.

THE RAISING OF LAZARUS
Etching of 1642 (Bredius 72)

Rembrandt has grasped that faith is the true
miracle: 'He that believeth on me, though he
die, yet shall he live.'

John 11.25

VII

CHRIST AT EMMAUS

Painting of 1629 (Bredius 539)

In this early work, Rembrandt tells the simple
story of St Luke in the style of his youthful
idea of 'natural liveliness'.

VIII

CHRIST AT EMMAUS

Painting about 1661 (Bredius 597)

It is all silence, but in this silence the truly
decisive thing happens: 'And their eyes were
opened, and they knew him.'

Luke 24.31

IX

VIRGIN AND CHILD SEATED ON THE CLOUDS

Etching by Federigo Barocci

This glorification of the Madonna in her angelic sweetness is a true product of the spirit and art of the Counter-Reformation.

X

VIRGIN AND CHILD SEATED ON THE CLOUDS

Etching of 1641 (Bredius 61)

Rembrandt at the crossroads. 'But Mary kept all these sayings, pondering them in her heart.' This biblical substance effects us more powerfully in this picture than the mannerism borrowed from the baroque style.

THE ANNUNCIATION

Drawing about 1645 (Valentiner 287)

The angel said: 'Hail, thou that art highly
favoured, the Lord is with thee. But she was
greatly troubled at the saying, and cast in her
mind what manner of salutation this might be.
And the angel said unto her, Fear not, Mary
. . . behold, thou shalt conceive in thy womb,
and bring forth a son. . . .'

Luke 1.28-31

XII

THE PRESENTATION IN THE TEMPLE

Drawing about 1645 (Valentiner 314)

Simeon 'blessed God, and said, Now lettest thou thy servant depart, O Lord, according to thy word, in peace; For mine eyes have seen thy salvation. . . .'

Luke 2.28-29

XIII

CHRIST RETURNING FROM THE TEMPLE WITH HIS PARENTS

Etching of 1654 (Bredius 60)

'His mother said unto him, Son, why hast thou
thus dealt with us? . . . And he said unto them,
How is it that ye sought me? wist ye not that
I must be in my Father's house? And they
understood not the saying . . . His mother kept
all these sayings in her heart.'

Luke 2.48-51

XIV

THE TEMPTATION OF JESUS

Drawing about 1652 (Valentiner 357)

'Again, the devil taketh him unto an exceeding high mountain, and sheweth him all the kingdoms of the world, and the glory of them; And he said unto him, All these things will I give thee, if thou wilt fall down and worship me. Then saith Jesus unto him, Get thee hence, Satan: for it is written, Thou shalt worship the Lord thy God, and him only shalt thou serve.'

Matt. 4.8-10

XV

CHRIST WALKING ON THE WAVES

Drawing about 1655 (Valentiner 426)

'Peter . . . walked upon the waters . . . But when he saw the wind, he was afraid; and beginning to sink, he cried out, saying, Lord, save me. And immediately Jesus stretched forth his hand, and took hold of him.'

Matt. 14.29-31

XVI

CHRIST WASHING THE APOSTLES' FEET

Drawing about 1658 (Valentiner 444)

'Peter saith unto him, Thou shalt never wash my feet. Jesus answered him, If I wash thee not, thou hast no part with me. Simon Peter saith unto him, Lord, not my feet only, but also my hands and my head.'

John 13.8-9

XVII

CHRIST IN GETHSEMANE

Drawing about 1655 (Valentiner 451)

'And he was parted from them about a stone's cast; and he kneeled down and prayed, Saying, Father, if thou be willing, remove this cup from me: nevertheless not my will, but thine, be done.'

Luke 22.41-2

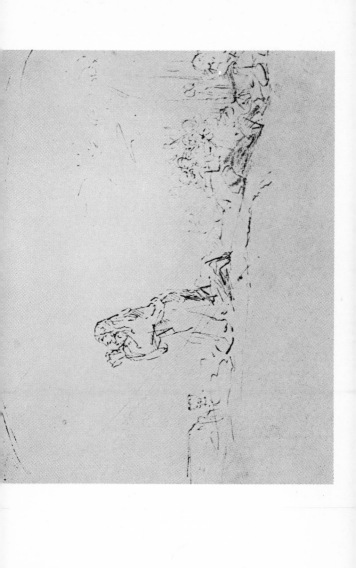

XVIII

CHRIST IN GETHSEMANE

Drawing about 1657 (Valentiner 452)

'And there appeared unto him an angel from heaven, strengthening him. And being in an agony he prayed more earnestly: and his sweat became as it were great drops of blood falling down upon the ground.'

Luke 22.43-4

XIX

CHRIST IN GETHSEMANE
Etching about 1657 (Bredius 75)

In this rendering of Luke 22. 43-4, 'the whole creation groaneth and travaileth in pain together until now.'

Rom. 8.22

CHRIST IN GETHSEMANE

Drawing about 1655 (Valentiner 450)

'And he cometh, and findeth them sleeping, and saith unto Peter, Simon, sleepest thou? couldest thou not watch one hour? Watch and pray, that ye enter not into temptation.'

Mark 14.37-8

THE ENTOMBMENT OF CHRIST

Etching about 1645 (Bredius 84)

Joseph of Arimathaea 'laid him in a tomb that was hewn in stone' . . . 'And there came also Nicodemus' . . . 'And the women which had come with him out of Galilee, followed after, and beheld the tomb, and how his body was laid.'

Luke 23.53, 55; John 19.39

CHRIST APPEARING TO HIS DISCIPLES

Drawing about 1648 (Valentiner 361)

'Jesus came and stood in the midst, and saith
unto them . . . As the Father hath sent me,
even so send I you.'

John 20.19-21

CHRIST AT EMMAUS

Copy of an original about 1655 (Valentiner 524)

'And it came to pass, while they communed
and questioned together, that Jesus himself
drew near, and went with them. But their eyes
were holden that they should not know him.'

Luke 24.15-16

THE ADORATION OF THE SHEPHERDS WITH THE LAMP

Etching about 1654 (Bredius 45)

The shepherds 'came with haste, and found both Mary and Joseph, and the babe lying in the manger. And when they saw it, they made known concerning the saying which was spoken to them about this child. . . . But Mary kept all these sayings, pondering them in her heart.'

Luke 2.16-19

XXV

THE ADORATION OF
THE MAGI

Painting of 1657 (Bredius 592)

'And when they saw the star, they rejoiced with exceeding great joy. And they came into the house and saw the young child with Mary his mother; and they fell down and worshipped him; and opening their treasures they offered unto him gifts. . . .'

Matt. 2.10-11

XXVI

JOSEPH'S DREAM IN
BETHLEHEM

Painting of 1645 (Bredius 569)

'Behold, an angel of the Lord appeared to Joseph in a dream, saying, Arise and take the young child and his mother, and flee into Egypt, and be thou there until I tell thee.'

Matt. 2.13

XXVII

JOSEPH'S DREAM IN EGPYT
Drawing about 1650 (Valentiner 333)

'But when Herod was dead, behold, an angel
of the Lord appeareth in a dream to Joseph
in Egypt, Saying, Arise and take the young
child and his mother, and go into the land of
Israel: for they are dead that sought the young
child's life.'

Matt. 2.19-20

MATTHEW 19
(THE HUNDRED GUILDER PRINT)

Etching about 1649 (Bredius 74)

The whole 19th chapter of St. Matthew's
Gospel: the sick, the Pharisees, the children,
the rich young man, and in their midst he on
whom everything depends.

NATHAN AND DAVID

Drawing about 1663 (Valentiner 167)

'And Nathan said to David, Thou art the man. . . . Wherefore hast thou despised the word of the Lord?'

II Sam. 12.7, 9

XXX

NATHAN AND DAVID

Drawing about 1663 (Valentiner 168)

'And David said unto Nathan, I have sinned against the Lord.'

II Sam. 12.13

XXXI
DAVID IN PRAYER
Etching of 1652 (Bredius 41)

'And the Lord struck the child . . . David
therefore besought God for the child . . . and
went in, and lay all night upon the earth.'

II Sam. 12.15-16

XXXII

THE EVANGELIST MATTHEW
Painting of 1661 (Bredius 614)

'So belief cometh of hearing.'

Rom. 10.17

'For we cannot but speak the things which we saw and heard.'

Acts 4.20